Best W[ishes]

1909

MW01285713

This
you know
where abouts.
to hear from
sorry that I did
to be with you
ather evenning
thing to tell
leaves me

ay be used for writing

POST CARD
THIS HALF FOR ADDRESS
ATLANTIC CITY
12 M
1910

Miss Emma
Kenet Sq
Ba[r]

bout quit roaming
ummer, I did go
chester on my way
ope you all are
a pleasant time
city.

st
es!

Miss Emma

Emma's
Postcard Album

ATLANTIC
MIGRATIONS
— AND THE —
AFRICAN
DIASPORA

Jessica B. Harris, Series Editor

The University Press of Mississippi is the scholarly publishing agency of the Mississippi Institutions of Higher Learning: Alcorn State University, Delta State University, Jackson State University, Mississippi State University, Mississippi University for Women, Mississippi Valley State University, University of Mississippi, and University of Southern Mississippi.

www.upress.state.ms.us

The University Press of Mississippi is a member of the Association of University Presses.

Library of Congress Cataloging-in-Publication Data

Names: Mitchell, Faith, 1952– author.
Title: Emma's postcard album : Black lives in the early twentieth century / Faith Mitchell.
Other titles: Atlantic migrations and the African diaspora.
Description: Jackson : University Press of Mississippi, [2023] | Series: Atlantic migrations and the african diaspora | Includes bibliographical references and index.
Identifiers: LCCN 2022024351 (print) | LCCN 2022024352 (ebook) | ISBN 9781496843159 (hardback) | ISBN 9781496843173 (epub) | ISBN 9781496843203 (epub) | ISBN 9781496843180 (pdf) | ISBN 9781496843197 (pdf)
Subjects: LCSH: African Americans—History—20th century. | African American families—History—20th century. | African Americans—Social conditions—History—20th century. | African Americans—Social life and customs—20th century. | African American women—History—20th century. | African Americans—History—Pictorial works. | African Americans in art—20th century. | Postcards—United States—History—20th century.
Classification: LCC E185.86 .M567 2023 (print) | LCC E185.86 (ebook) | DDC 973/.049607300904—dc23/eng/20220629
LC record available at https://lccn.loc.gov/2022024351
LC ebook record available at https://lccn.loc.gov/2022024352

British Library Cataloging-in-Publication Data available

To Archie and Lex—and all those,
known and unknown,
whose vision and strength
made a way for us.

Herein lie buried many things which if read with patience may show the strange meaning of being Black here in the dawning of the Twentieth Century.
—W. E. B. Du Bois, Introduction, *The Souls of Black Folk*

Contents

Emma's
Postcard Album

Emma Victoria Crawford, c. 1906.

Emma Crawford's
Postcard Collection

The story of this book begins, like many a good adventure, with a hidden treasure. After my mother's death, I discovered, in the trunk that served as her personal archive, a carefully preserved album of turn-of-the-century postcards—*her* mother Emma's collection from her young adulthood. At first I simply admired the array of beautiful cards, but I was increasingly curious about the story behind them. Who sent them to Emma, my grandmother? Why was she moving around so often, with different addresses? What could the postcards tell me about not just her life but also the larger story of her people, place, and time? We know so little about the everyday lives of Black Americans across the generations; could the cards tell more?

This book is the result of my questioning. It tells the story of a Black family within the larger setting of their times, using my grandmother's postcard collection as a window on the world of a century ago. Bringing the story to life involved years of scholarly and genealogical research, undergirded by anthropological training that guided me to look at the social and cultural significance of what I encountered. Throughout, I was driven by the desire to tell the story of Black life in a particular time and place, knowing that there aren't enough stories of Black life as it has been lived in our four-hundred-plus years on this continent. Unfortunately, there will never be enough; too many people were rendered voiceless by slavery and racism. Every contribution is therefore vital for broadening and deepening our understanding of the Black American experience.

My research started with oral history. I grew up with my mother's stories about our forebears' lives as free Black families in rural Pennsylvania. Like a griot, she repeated them often, used them as life lessons, and tested my ability to remember the details, no doubt echoing the way the stories had been passed down to her by her own mother. Because the generations in the family are long and family members lived in proximity for many decades, her stories included firsthand accounts from long before my time. Thus, the past never seemed as distant to me as it might to some, and it was alive with people and events that held personal significance.

Importantly, these stories affirmed that our family and other Black people were a part of American history, whether this role was formally acknowledged or not. Reflecting on this now, I see how such affirmations were one of the ways these earlier generations kept their heads above the water in a racist society. They prized their personal experiences and used the stories about the wars they'd fought in, the churches they'd built, the places where they'd worked, and what they thought about the white people they'd worked for to build and maintain a system of sustaining values that countered their poverty and social marginalization. These were some of the practices that enabled Black Americans to nurture a sense of agency over the decades—agency among themselves that was both unrecognized by, and unacceptable to, the larger society.

James Baldwin described this sense of quiet authority beautifully: "That man who is forced each day to snatch his manhood, his identity, out of the fire of human cruelty that rages to destroy it knows . . . something about himself and human life that no school on earth—and, indeed, no church—can teach. He achieves his own authority, and that is unshakable."[1]

◆　◆　◆

At the outset of this project, I knew little about deltiology, as the study and collection of postcards is known. My interest in Emma's postcards was primarily from the perspective of Black history. However, as my research continued, it became clear to me that although there were many books *about* postcards, there were few examples of what I was trying to do, which was to examine postcards in a broader context and use their text not only as personal narrative but also as reflective of social history. In fact, as I subsequently learned, opportunities to analyze original postcard collections within specific biographical contexts are quite rare.[2] This would be doubly true for African Americans, for whom personal narratives are sadly scarce.

Therefore, Emma's postcard collection is a genuine gift from the past. As snippets of lived experience, eye-catching visual images, and reflections of historical moments, the cards in it are sources for understanding not only African American life but also broader American history and culture. The original collection covers 1906 to 1916, the heyday of American post-card collecting, with the 1906–10 period discussed in these pages. This was the "golden age" of postcards, when they were beautifully designed to delight the eyes and imaginations of people who might never leave the small towns and villages where they grew up. Through the imagery of the cards, we are introduced to the sights, customs, and events of the vibrant early twentieth century, as selected by the cards' senders. Their choices represent tiny nuggets of personal meaning, reflecting what these senders found beautiful, interesting, humorous, or heartfelt. In addition, through the messages of the cards, we are brought into Emma's private world. Even when very short, these texts shed light on Black Americans' everyday lives.

Altogether, the collection adds to our understanding of the lived experience of Black women and Black families at a pivotal time in American history. A tiny minority in an overwhelmingly white state, Emma and her ancestors had withstood decades of hostility, mistreatment, and challenges to their freedom. The resources that they and other Black families relied on for survival, including ties of family and religion—and a relentless focus on education—are part of the story told by the postcards. In this way Emma's collection is the gateway to a racial story, one of painful struggle against racism's oppressions, of determined perseverance despite the odds, and of creating meaningful, often joyful, experiences in a difficult environment. Proudly and valiantly "made by themselves," as pioneering Black sociologist W. E. B. Du Bois brilliantly observed in 1900, the people we meet in these pages are "studying, examining, and thinking of their own progress and prospects," thereby carrying on the efforts of their forefathers and laying the groundwork for generations to come.[3]

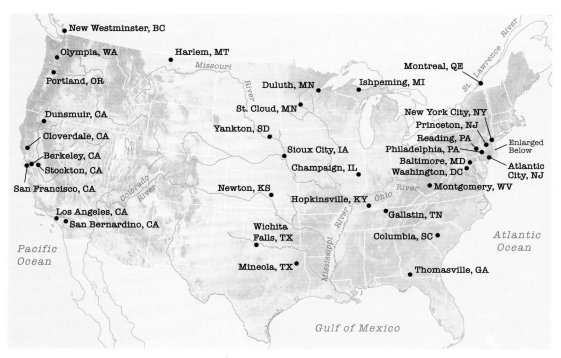

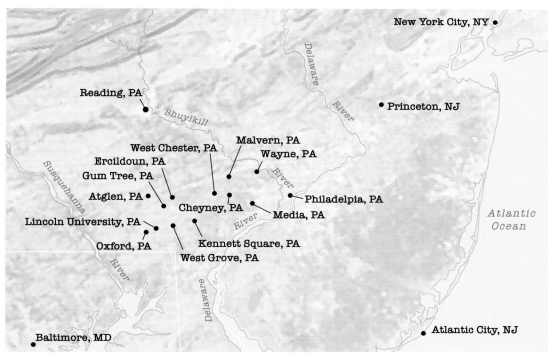

These maps show the towns and cities that Emma Crawford's postcards were mailed from or to. Many locations track with the travel routes of Richards & Pringle's Georgia Minstrels. Lincoln University, PA was Emma's home base.

Chapter One

What Stories Can Postcards Tell?

Postcards are part diary, part travel log, part visual reinterpretation of the experienced world. Through them, personal narratives merge with the larger historical picture. Thus, Emma Crawford's postcards, and the stories reflected in them, provide us with insights into how Black people shaped the intimate dimensions of their own lives as well as how Black people's lives were shaped by their times. Although Black Americans "were forced into segregation," novelist Ralph Ellison wrote, "within that situation we were able to live close to the larger society and to abstract from it enough combinations of values, including religion and hope and art, which allowed us to endure and impose our own idea of what the world should be, of what man should be, and of what American society should be."[1]

Emma's postcards help us understand what "our own idea of what the world should be" looked like a century ago in the everyday lives of people. The cards are insights into what historian Leon Litwack terms the "interior life, largely unknown and incomprehensible to whites [that permitted Black Americans] to survive and endure."[2] The difficulty of obtaining these insights should not be underestimated. For African Americans, the personal stories that could—and should—fill out the historic record are rare and difficult to know, because there have been so few diaries, letters, first-person narratives, or other personal documents to draw on, apart from the records of a few luminaries. Much Black storytelling is oral rather than written, and this was especially true a century ago. Literacy was limited, and even when there was a written record in letters and notebooks, these documents were easily lost over time, especially by a people on the move throughout the South as well as out of the South and into other states. As a result, we have limited access to the lived sense of the era and to the pace and shape of people's lives.

This is one of the contributions of Emma's postcard collection. The cards are an insight into Black Americans at work—what people did, where they did it, and for whom—and into their family life. They are from a musician traveling across the country with minstrel shows and introducing remote small towns to ragtime; from friends and relatives working in other states or the next town over; and from suitors for Emma's hand. They show us how people communicated across the miles: what they wrote each other about, and how they expressed their ideas. There is teasing, warmth, flirtation, and there are expressions of sisterhood and familial affection.

The postcard collection itself was a sign of the times. Emma began collecting cards during a period when postcard collecting had become wildly popular, following the introduction of postcards to American audiences at the World's Columbian Exposition in Chicago in 1893.[3] Clubs were organized to promote "philocarty" or "cartephilia" (now encompassed in the preferred term "deltiology"), and it was said that "every little town has several exclusive post-card stores, and the cities have more post-card stores than grocery stores."[4] For small-town merchants and retail outlets, postcards were attractive because they required small amounts of display space and turned a good profit. For postcard collectors, the hobby was addictive, because cards were inexpensive, reflected a variety of topics, and could be exchanged and discussed with friends and relatives. Typically organized into an album that would be prominently displayed at home, postcards were a source of entertainment in an era without radio and with little competition from still-developing vinyl recordings and movies.[5] They enabled people to temporarily escape the limitations of narrow home lives to trace their fingers across a "viewable, purchasable, pleasurable world."[6]

In 1908 close to 670 million cards were mailed in the US alone. At first, postal regulations permitted only the name and address of the recipient to be written on the back, so messages were limited to the illustrated side. After 1907 messages could be written on the back of the card. This enhanced the use of postcards for informal communication, especially in larger cities, where mail was delivered several times a day. In the small towns where Emma lived, mail deliveries were less frequent—but still took place once or twice daily—making postcards effective for quick conversational updates.

Postcard publishers endeavored not only to sell cards that covered a variety of subjects but also to make the cards aesthetically appealing. Until 1909 most postcards were imported from Germany, where lithographic techniques were superior, and painstaking workmanship was very cheap. After tariff legislation favoring American postcard production was enacted in 1909, the aesthetic quality of cards gradually deteriorated, because the American printers and publishers could not match the high quality of German lithography. This development contributed to declining interest in postcard collecting, following a final peak of interest in 1913.[7]

Picture postcards in the early twentieth century "thoroughly and relentlessly captured the era in a manner that reveals a better portrait of this age

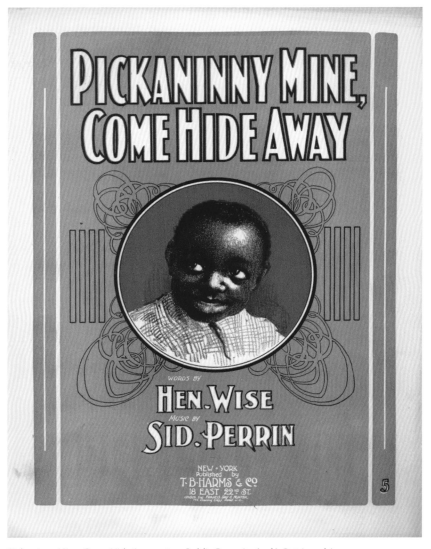

Pickaninny Mine, Come Hide Away, 1899. Public Domain. (n.d.). Retrieved January 11, 2022, from The Library of Congress, Performing Arts Databases, http://memory.loc.gov/diglib/ihas/loc.award.rpbaasm.0855/default.html.

than of most others," notes postcard historian Dorothy B. Ryan.[8] This is certainly true of Emma's collection, where her times are reflected in artistic cards produced by master German printers, in noticeably cruder American cards, and in cards that capture the evolving technology and architecture of the day. The collection captures the energy and optimism of a period when the United States was emerging as a world power and an industrial giant.[9]

There is only one "Black" card in Emma's collection, "Darktown Doctors" from 1907 (see chapter 3), but several kinds of postcards with images

HORSE SHOE FALL FROM BELOW NIAGARA FALLS

Horse Shoe Fall from below Niagara Falls

of Black people were circulated in this period. One type, like "Darktown Doctors," reflected racist stereotypes that were widespread in white popular culture. Such images depicted Black people as foolish at best and criminal at worst. It was the era of the "coon"—pejoratively short for "raccoon"—a lazy, easily frightened, chronically idle, inarticulate buffoon who was memorialized in song, on the stage, in visual imagery and material objects, and in everyday language.[10] Other common visual stereotypes were Mammy, who was obese and maternal, and the pickaninny, a child with bulging eyes who was often depicted eating watermelon (see chapter 5 for more on this topic).

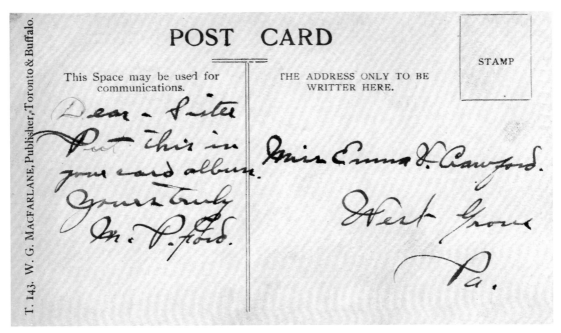

"Dear Sister, Put this in your card album. Yours truly, M. P. Ford" (Emma's brother Merris's stage name).

An unmailed card that had perhaps been enclosed in a letter, addressed to Emma at an address in West Grove, Pennsylvania, most likely the Milton C. Pyle household. Postcard publisher: W. G. MacFarlane, Toronto and Buffalo, T. 143. Where known, the card title, mailing date, and publisher will be noted.

Another racist stereotype, that of the savage, animalistic, and criminal Black brute, was the subject of a second type of postcard, the lynching photograph. In 1911 the National Association for the Advancement of Colored People (NAACP) estimated that more than two thousand Black men had been lynched without trial since the 1880s.[11] The photographs and postcards of those lynchings, as Anthony W. Lee writes, "often pictured not only the mutilated and dangling bodies of the lynched victims but also, all too frequently, the proud, laughing, self-righteous crowds who attended and participated in the lynchings."[12] The images were intended to demonstrate white solidarity, to affirm white racial superiority, and to oppose Black advancement.[13] In 1908 the federal government tried to disrupt the distribution of lynching postcards by passing an amendment to postal law that prohibited mailing items "tending to incite arson, murder or assassination." However, the unintended effect of the law was mainly to drive the circulation of these cards underground.[14]

A third kind of postcard was produced specifically for Black audiences with the intention of disrupting the prevailing racism. For example, in 1908 educator and feminist Nannie Helen Burroughs began producing dolls, postcards, and calendars with positive Black images. *The Indi-anapolis Freeman*, a national Black newspaper, reported that she did this having seen that "progressive, race-loving Negroes . . . had grown tired of the 'piccaninnies, water melon eating, dice-throwing gang, and the gold dust twins burlesque." The article did not provide details about Burroughs's postcards, but her calendars were described as "the first high-class Negro calendars ever made in America or in the world, for that matter."[15] C. M. Battey, Tuskegee Institute's official photographer, also produced postcards and prints, using them to publicize his portraits of Black notables; other photographers may have done so as well.[16]

Rather than perpetuate racist imagery, the senders and recipients in Emma's circle chose alternative imagery: rosy-cheeked white children, cheery sentiments, and local landmarks, having many attractive options to choose from. The images were not "Black," but everything else about them—the senders, recipients, and messages—in some way reflected the Black experience. Through the brief messages of these postcard exchanges, we gain a sense of the spirit that enabled Emma, her friends and family, and other Black Americans to persevere and derive personal and collective meaning from their lives, despite living in a period that was deeply hostile to their integrity and aspirations.

A visually dazzling journey into a world we know far too little about awaits. Let us begin!

Chapter Two

The Status of the Negro in This Country

The turn of the twentieth century—an era of unfettered Jim Crow racism—sets the stage for the stories told by Emma Crawford's postcards, whose friendly, lighthearted messages and images belie the desperate nature of life during this period for Black Americans. Forty years after Emancipation, the rights Black people had achieved during the Reconstruction period had been systematically and brutally stripped away. Although Black Americans lived in one of the world's wealthiest countries—in 1900 US GDP per capita was the world's third highest[1]—they were locked out of full participation in it. Black communities were under assault from domestic terrorism, and Black leaders were torn about the right course for achieving social progress and preventing further losses. These circumstances shaped every aspect of Black existence reflected in the postcards: schooling, family and community life, and working in the white world.

This period was so problematic for Black Americans that it is customarily referred to as the nadir of Black history.[2] Legal segregation in both northern and southern states was reinforced by mass mob violence against Black communities, disenfranchisement of the Black vote, and unchecked lynching of Black men. W. E. B. Du Bois once described seeing the dried fingers of a recently lynched Black man on display in the front of an Atlanta grocery—a presumably "ordinary" reminder for the grocery's customers and passersby of this central ritual of racial control.[3]

About the 1900–1910 period, the National Association for the Advancement of Colored People (NAACP) wrote in 1911,

We have seen wholesale disfranchisement of colored voters, color caste carried to the point of positive cruelty, the rule of the mob and the lynching of 2,000 men [since 1885] without legal trial, growing discrimination in schools, travel, and public conveniences, and an openly declared determination to stop the development of millions of men at the dead line of color.[4]

The Man in the Moon Is a Coon.—"Coon" imagery in sheet music (1895). George M. Cohan. *The Man in the Moon Is a Coon.* New York: Howley, Haviland. Retrieved from https://doi.org/10.5479/sil.982148.mq1687926.

But while white supremacy ruled supreme—as both custom and law—challenges to it were beginning to take shape. One of these was the Niagara Movement, first organized in 1905 and committed to full citizenship rights for Black Americans. Another was the NAACP, established in 1909 with the mission of championing equal rights and eliminating racial prejudice.[5] Reflecting this rising spirit of change and challenge, Du Bois, who was a founding member of both organizations, presciently observed in 1900 that "the problem of the twentieth century is the problem of the color line."[6]

. . . and in a national cartoon, *The Hoodoo Coon and The Black Cat* (1906). *The Idaho Springs Sifting-News*. (1906, September 1). Retrieved July 14, 2020, from Library of Congress, Chronicling America: https://chroniclingamerica .loc.gov/lccn/sn90051006/1906-09-01/ed-1/seq-4/.

At the century's opening, Americans, both Black and white, were predominantly rural. Most Black families still lived in the former slave states of the South, where peonage, sharecropping, and tenant farming confined them to conditions that were close to slavery.[7] About a fifth of them were former slaves, and many were just a generation removed from bondage.[8] The majority of Black men were agricultural workers, while most Black women were employed in domestic and personal service (washing, cooking, cleaning, taking care of children).[9]

Average Black life expectancy was a short thirty-four years. Whites lived on average more than a decade longer, to forty-eight years.[10] Forty-five percent of Black adults were illiterate, and despite having a deep hunger for education, many families had limited access to schooling for their children.[11] The movement of millions of southern Black people and families to southern cities as well as to the West and urban North in search of a better way of life was still a decade away.

Among white Americans of the period, it was commonly believed that African Americans were inferior, unattractive, dirty, and unintelligent.[12] Popular imagery relentlessly reinforced this message—and no other one. Black men and women were perceived, and depicted, exclusively as servants, laborers, criminals, ignorant southern darkies, and other undesirable types.

Black people who aspired to improve their status were ridiculous social climbers. Black women were singled out as being debased and immoral, the antithesis of virtuous and sheltered white women. "Nowhere in the civilized world can there be found a more forlorn spectacle than [a Black] woman," one observer wrote in 1899. "She becomes any man's mistress, every man's victim. To speak of a Negro woman's virtue is to excite a smile."[13]

Emma, her family members, and friends constantly confronted and fought these stereotypes. Their struggle was to claim individuality in a society in which their hopes, dreams, and deeper lives were unrecognized and unvalued. Success would be measured by their ability to keep their heads up—by fighting poverty and servility, maintaining some level of personal integrity, and sustaining a sense of purpose.

The Fall from Reconstruction

"The South is attempting to crush the manhood and self-respect out of the negro; the South is determined to smile upon the servile, fawning, cowardly and sicofantine [sic] negro and to frown upon the brave, manly, and aggressive negro," the *Colored American Magazine* asserted in 1900. It continued:

> The South is bent upon a policy of extermination or subjugation; they will either exterminate the negro or subjugate him. Fifteen hundred negroes have been lynched since the year 1890, and only one tenth of them have been charged with the unspeakable crime of outrage upon defenseless women. The supreme court of the United States permits laws to be passed against the negro which are contrary to the spirit of the Fourteenth and Fifteenth Amendments. In the North many of the northern pulpits are silent, and there seems to be a strange apathy and indifference at the attempt of the South to crush the manhood and self-respect out of the negro.[14]

This 1900 editorial captures turn-of-the-century Black outrage about the resurgence of white supremacy and accompanying erosion of Black civil rights following the end of Reconstruction ("the spirit of the Fourteenth and Fifteenth Amendments" refers to citizenship and voting rights, respectively). Early twentieth-century "Jim Crow" laws were soon to follow, resulting in legal segregation in every imaginable domain of life—education, transportation systems, housing, public accommodations, and so forth—even in northern states, where the relatively small Black population posed no material threat to whites. Consequently, Emma Crawford faced as much discrimination in her Pennsylvania small town as any young Black girl in the South.

The arc from Reconstruction to Jim Crow began with the defeat of the Confederacy in 1865 and the federal government's subsequent effort "to redress the inequities of slavery and its political, social, and economic legacy and to solve the problems arising from the readmission to the Union of the 11 states that had seceded at or before the outbreak of war."[15] For a brief period of less than twenty years, the South flirted with the principle of racial equality—and achieved some notable accomplishments—before the resurgence of white supremacy reversed much of the progress that had been made.

The early phase of Reconstruction established for the first time in American history that Black people were citizens who were guaranteed equal rights under the US Constitution. Exercising their new right to vote and hold political office, more than a thousand Black men eventually secured elected positions in the South. Meanwhile, coalitions of white and Black reformers established the South's first public school systems and numerous charitable institutions.[16] Between 1861 and 1870, the American Missionary Association founded seven Black colleges and thirteen normal (teacher training) schools in southern states. Many of these institutions—along with private historically Black colleges and universities founded in later years—became the backbone of Black higher education, producing leaders for generations to come.

Reconstruction gave Black Americans a taste of full citizenship and held out the promise of ending, or limiting, their social and economic marginalization. However, the experiment abruptly ended in 1877, with the removal of federal troops from the South during the administration of President Rutherford Hayes. Subsequently, local rule in southern states returned to the hands of the former Confederates, and henceforth—until the civil rights era nearly one hundred years later—the federal government assumed a hands-off policy toward the "Negro problem."

With the end of a federal presence, the political and social gains the emancipated slaves had made during Reconstruction evaporated under the assault of white supremacists who used a variety of illegal practices to reduce the former slaves to second-class citizenship and deprive them of constitutionally guaranteed civil and human rights.[17]

The fall from Reconstruction's aspirations was exacerbated by President Andrew Johnson's earlier 1865 order that returned land that had previously been in federal hands to its white former owners. The emancipated slaves' dream of "40 acres and a mule" thereby died before it could ever materialize. Without land, most were forced back into working on white plantations. Henceforth, and for many decades that followed, most southern Black people were landless and poor.[18]

The nineteenth century ended with the Supreme Court's 1896 *Plessy v. Ferguson* decision, which dealt a final blow to Black Americans' goal of racial equality. The decision's assertion that state segregation laws were constitutional, so long as Black Americans were provided "separate but equal" facilities, fueled the deterioration of Black rights and opportunities throughout the country.

Domestic Terrorism

Mob violence accompanied the early twentieth-century deterioration in Black civil rights, with several major racial disturbances and numerous smaller ones taking place during the first decade. Their effect was to sow fear, destroy visible Black achievements, such as stores and homes, and cement the subordinate status of families and communities. Hundreds of Black men were also lynched during this period.[19] As a result, Black families and communities lived in constant fear, vulnerable to unsubstantiated rumors and to the violent impulses of angry white mobs, with no protection from the police or courts. In every instance of racial violence, whites were the aggressors, usually acting in response to an alleged assault on an innocent white citizen, especially a white woman. In the case of the dozens of riots that followed Jack Johnson's 1910 boxing victory over James Jeffries (the "Great White Hope"), Black celebrations were the triggering events.[20]

Violence against Black people was tolerated by sheriffs and police—and abetted by them in several cases. The white press played an active role, frequently referring to the "race war," and publishing headlines like "RACE FEELING GROWS INTENSE—WHITES SAY ALL NEGROES MUST GO," which appeared in the Augusta, Georgia, *Chronicle* in April 1906.[21] The attacks were the product of multiple toxic factors operating in concert, including the prevailing racism of the day, widely held sexual stereotypes about Black men lusting after white women, and underlying fears about Black communities' economic and political progress, both real and perceived. For example, while whites rationalized lynching as a means of protecting the violated honor of innocent white women, it also functioned to keep individual Black people and Black communities subservient, and to control the Black labor force. In his introduction to Walter White's comprehensive study of lynching for the NAACP, Kenneth R. Janken observed that "between 1890 and 1930 [lynching] was used with a high level of frequency to keep African Americans in their place by policing racial boundaries, punishing and terrorizing prosperous African Americans, and squelching hints of Black opposition to the racial order."[22]

Domestic racial terrorism killed hundreds of innocent people, tore apart Black families, crippled the development of communities, and deepened racial divides. From the many incidents in the first decade of the twentieth century, two examples—the 1906 race riot in Atlanta, Georgia, and the 1908 riot in Springfield, Illinois—well illustrate motivations and outcomes in action.

In September 1906 Atlanta's Black residents were attacked for three days following unsubstantiated rumors in local newspapers about Black men assaulting white women. The violence began on September 22, when an angry crowd of nearly ten thousand white men and boys gathered on Decatur Street in the downtown Atlanta area of Five Points. At some point, a white police officer shot into the roiling mass of people. His gunfire was returned, and in the resulting chaos, one officer was killed and another one was wounded. These events were the impetus for a general destruction of Black life and property by the white mob. The houses of Black residents were looted and burned, and for several days the city was paralyzed. The *Indianapolis Freeman* reported, "Unoffending Negroes have been snatched from street cars, beaten to death, and many have been wounded with probable fatal results. Hundreds have fled to the surrounding country for their lives."[23]

In the aftermath of the riot, the official count was that twenty-five Black people had died and one white, but unofficially, more than one hundred people may have been killed.[24] No action was brought against any of the white rioters.[25]

Two years later the 1908 Springfield, Illinois, riot led to the deaths of five whites and two Black people, as well as significant material damage to homes and businesses in the Black community. In the usual pattern, the rationale was the alleged assault of a white woman by a Black man. Deeper in the background were social tensions generated by growing Black political power and ongoing competition between Black laborers and recent European immigrants for low-wage jobs.[26]

Mabel Hallam's claim that she had been raped the night before by a Black man was the spark for the violence. "The fellow dragged me into the back yard," she said, "carrying and pulling me through the kitchen in our home. He pulled and jerked and yanked at me until we were in one of the outbuildings. All the time his fingers were being buried into my neck and the pain was intense." Mabel soon identified George Richardson, a Black construction laborer, who had been working on a house not far from her house, as her rapist. "Before God, I am innocent of this crime," Richardson insisted. "I can explain her identification of me only by the theory that all coons look alike to her." Within fifteen minutes of Mabel's arrival at the courthouse to identify her assailant, a crowd had formed in downtown Springfield.[27]

The white mob eventually traveled to the Levee, a predominantly African American area, where they destroyed numerous Black-owned businesses. After unsuccessfully attempting to disperse the rioters, the governor called out the militia. Meanwhile, more than two thousand Black people left the city, and hundreds fled to the militia's camps, as whites began systematically destroying Black homes. It took two days, and militia-patrolled streets, to restore order. Ultimately, the men who were believed to have led the riot escaped punishment. In addition, members of the white community engaged in a political and economic boycott to drive out Springfield's remaining Black residents.[28]

Although Mabel Hallam confessed to a grand jury two weeks after the riot that her story was a lie, she was never held accountable for her behavior or its aftermath. In fact, only a single white rioter suffered serious punishment for his role in the violence. Nevertheless, the riot represented a kind of turning point for Black communities, for concern about both its destructiveness and its location in a northern city eventually contributed to the formation of the National Association for the Advancement of Colored People (NAACP) in 1909.[29]

Immediately after the Springfield riot, Booker T. Washington—known for typically holding conciliatory racial views—published an open letter appealing for a return to the rule of law. His letter provides additional evidence about the flimsy rationales used to justify killing Black men and illustrates the public element that was an important aspect of lynch mobs.

> Baltimore, Aug. 19—Within the past sixty days twenty-five Negroes have been lynched in different parts of the United States. Of this number only four were even charged with criminal assault upon women. Nine were lynched in one day on the charge of being connected with murder. Four were lynched in one day on the charge that they passed resolutions in a lodge approving the murder of an individual. Three were lynched in one day on the charge that they had taken part in the burning of a gin house. The others were lynched for miscellaneous reasons.
>
> One was publicly burned in open daylight in the presence of women and children, after oil had been poured upon his body, at Greenville, Tex., and reports state that a thousand people witnessed the spectacle in the open square of the town. One other victim was eighty years of age. How long can our Christian civilization stand this? I am making no special plea for the Negro, innocent or guilty, but I am calling attention to the danger that threatens our civilization.[30]

Black newspapers joined Booker T. Washington in decrying the absence of the rule of law and the punishment of whole communities for the alleged actions of a few—but to little avail. Although two hundred antilynching bills were brought before Congress in the first half of the twentieth century, white southern interests successfully fought these efforts. It was not until 2022, more than a century later, that the Emmett Till Antilynching Act made lynching a federal hate crime, punishable by up to thirty years in prison.[31]

Uplifting the Race

Despite the atmosphere of violence and the virtually insurmountable social and economic obstacles they confronted, Black Americans nevertheless made gradual progress during the beginning decades of the twentieth century. For example, although Black children's access to education was still sharply limited compared to that of white children, illiteracy dropped from 61 to 33 percent between 1890 and 1910, while life expectancy at birth increased by thirteen years for males and nine years for females in the decade between 1909–11 and 1919–21.[32]

Emma Crawford was a product of these changing times, as will be seen. Her educational goals, interest in being a nurse, choice of companions, and identification with Black Victorian standards of behavior all reflected her attraction to the new Black world that was taking shape and the values of self-improvement and respectability that dominated social rhetoric.

Black advancement evolved dramatically in cities—even before the massive movement of Black Americans from rural communities to northern, midwestern, and western cities during the Great Migration. At the turn of the century, there were ten southern cities with ten thousand or more Black residents—Atlanta, Baltimore, Charleston, Louisville, Memphis, Nashville, New Orleans, Richmond, St. Louis, and Washington DC—and three in the north: Chicago, New York, and Philadelphia. Within these urban areas, a small but growing Black professional class was taking shape, numbering teachers, professors, ministers, doctors, dentists, journalists, lawyers, actors, musicians, and photographers among its members. In the early years of the century, about two thousand Black men and women held college degrees, and there were four Black-owned banks.[33] "It is plain that there is a steady increase of college-bred Negroes from decade to decade," Du Bois reported in 1900. "There is today about one college trained person in every 3,600 Negroes."[34]

This nascent middle class was the focus of a fierce debate among Black political and social leaders about the proper course for Black progress. At the beginning of the century, Booker T. Washington, the former slave who had founded Tuskegee Normal School for Colored Teachers (later

Booker T. Washington, 1856–1915, in 1903. Library of Congress. (n.d.). *Prints & Photographs Online Catalogue*. Retrieved April 20, 2020, from https://memory.loc.gov/pnp/cph/3a40000/3a49000/3a49600/3a49671r.jpg.

Tuskegee Institute, and now Tuskegee University) in 1881, held sway. Promoting a philosophy of racial accommodation and dedication to vocational training, Washington saw the solution to "the Negro problem" as resting in self-improvement and self-help. He minimized the impact of segregation and placed full responsibility on Black Americans for the improvement of their quality of life and status relative to whites. Comfortable with Washington's unthreatening vision, whites dubbed him "the national Negro leader."[35]

In Washington's view the surest way for Black people to gain equal social rights was to demonstrate "industry, thrift, intelligence and property." For example, in 1896 he confidently asserted, "It is through the dairy farm, the truck garden, the trades, and commercial life, largely, that the negro is to find his way to the enjoyment of all his rights. Whether he will or not, a white man respects a negro who owns a two-story brick house."[36]

An essential element of his thinking—known generally as the Tuskegee philosophy—was that while Black Americans were entitled to free basic education, their instruction should be limited to vocational or industrial training, for instance, as teachers or nurses. Meanwhile, they should not press for the right to vote, should tolerate segregation and discrimination, and should not retaliate against racist behavior.

Washington's influential "Atlanta Compromise" speech on September 18, 1895—just a year before *Plessy v. Ferguson*—famously promised a predominantly white audience, "In all things that are purely social [the races]

W. E. B. Du Bois, 1868–1963, in 1918. Library of Congress. (n.d.). *Prints & Photographs Online Catalogue*. Retrieved April 20, 2020, from W. E. B. (William Edward Burghardt) Du Bois, 1868–1963: http://loc.gov/pictures/resource/cph.3a53178/.

can be as separate as the fingers, yet one as the hand in all things essential to mutual progress."[37] This reassuring vision of shared advancement undergirded by rigid racial separation gained Washington enthusiastic support from whites, who were assured that there would be no challenges to the existing power structure.

About Washington's philosophy, Du Bois wrote, "It startled the nation to hear a Negro advocating such a program after many decades of bitter complaint; it startled and won the applause of the South, it interested and won the admiration of the North; and after a confused murmur of protest, it silenced if it did not convert the Negroes themselves."[38]

Du Bois himself had been an initial supporter of Washington's views. Like Washington, he had held Black people responsible for their social and economic condition, emphasized self-help and moral improvement, encouraged the development of Black business, and promoted industrial training for the Black masses.[39] However, by the early years of the new century, Du Bois was a strong critic of Washington and his influence. Notably, in 1903's *The Souls of Black Folk*, he wrote forcefully about his rejection of Washington's "gradual" approach to Black social integration and called instead for agitation on behalf of African American rights:

Is it possible, and probable, that nine millions of men can make effective progress in economic lines if they are deprived of political rights, made a servile caste, and allowed only the most meagre chance for developing their exceptional men? If history and reason give any distinct answer to these questions, it is an emphatic *No*.[40]

In 1905 Du Bois and journalist William Monroe Trotter organized a meeting of Black intellectuals and professionals in Niagara Falls, Canada, that paved the way for the legal challenges to segregation that would transform the country's race relations decades later. The principles of the Niagara Movement, as it came to be called, included civil liberties, education, health, and employment. In addition, for years Du Bois argued persuasively against Washington's focus on technical education, calling as well for the classical training of the "talented tenth" of the Black population who would then provide leadership for other members of the race.[41]

Though their methods differed, W. E. B. Du Bois and Booker T. Washington were united in their mission to "uplift the race," the watchword of the era. Along with other social leaders, they "employed a range of strategies—discursive, cultural, political—to convey a vision of uplift as racial progress, solidarity, self-improvement, respectability, Christian morality, and social mobility," as historian Renée Ater has written.[42] This vision permeated literature, visual imagery, and social mores. African Americans wanted whites to see them as they envisioned themselves to be: dignified, successful, educated, temperate, respectable, and modern—in hopes that those perceptions would open the door to social and economic progress.

There was a strong focus on individual behavior, specifically on demonstrating that African Americans could act in ways that "merited" equal treatment and rights. "We must discriminate against discrimination by making ourselves so respected that [discrimination] will be impossible," *Alexander's Magazine* advised in 1906.[43] For Emma Crawford and other young women, this thinking was a cornerstone of parental upbringing: acceptance by the wider society required self-respect. Self-respect and Black pride demanded temperance, morality, thrift, and irreproachable behavior.[44] Association with "immoral" people or behavior was to be avoided at all costs. Given prevailing perceptions of Black women—"She is seduced before she reaches the age of puberty," wrote conservative novelist Corra Mae Harris—and their vulnerability to the unwanted attentions of both Black and white men, there was extreme pressure on socially aspiring women to maintain standards of modesty and decorum.[45]

The program of the Third Atlanta Conference for the Study of the Negro Problems, held in 1898 under Du Bois's leadership, was a revealing reflection of the dominant philosophy of self-improvement and respectability. The subject of the conference—"The Efforts of Negroes for Their Own Social Betterment"—signaled its orientation. Horace Bumstead, president of Atlanta University, reinforced the theme in his opening remarks, observing "one great step toward the solution [of the Negro problem] is the independent study of the question by Negroes themselves and spontaneous efforts at reform." Conference papers continued the theme of self-improvement:

"Good Manners" by Mrs. G. S. King
"Children's Rights" by Mrs. S. S. Butler
"Cleanliness" by Mrs. M. A. Ross
"Maxims for Mothers" by Mrs. T. N. Chase
"The Care of Homes" by Miss Brittain
"Social Purity"—a tract by Prof. Eugene Harris.[46]

Throughout the proceedings, self-sufficiency was celebrated, undergirded by the implicit assumption that improved conditions for Black Americans could be achieved without changes, or challenges, to existing racial hierarchies.

Today, with a century's hindsight, we know that respectability and self-help alone did not substantially improve the social and economic position of Black Americans. No matter how respectably they carried themselves, Black people had no chance of being accepted into the mainstream of the white American middle class.[47] Instead, their messages about, and efforts for, advancement could be effective only within the marginalized, racially defined world to which segregation confined them. It was not until the United States itself underwent major changes, including an economic transformation from agriculture to industry, the migration of Black workers and families from the South to the North, new federal programs, and the legal victories of the modern civil rights movement, that Black people's status in the aggregate substantially improved.[48]

Paradoxically, because Black success threatened whites, achieving respectability and material progress actually raised the risk of attracting violence. "By making blacks more ambitious and less content with staying in their 'place,' by encouraging them to acquire the property and wealth said to be necessary to secure white recognition, the success ethic in many instances only exacerbated white fears and hostility," historian Leon Litwack noted.[49] The destruction of middle-class neighborhoods in the 1906 Atlanta and 1908 Springfield riots and the attack on the prosperous "Black Wall Street" community of Greenwood in the 1921 Tulsa massacre were just a few examples of this dynamic in action. Litwack quotes a Black lawyer who told an English visitor in 1909, "Thirty years ago . . . the prejudice was against the ignorant, shiftless and thriftless black; now it is against the thrifty and industrious, the refined and the cultured—against those, in a word, who come into competition with the middle-class white."[50]

A Nation within a Nation

Although blocked at every turn from full participation in American society, early twentieth-century Black Americans created their own world—a nation within a nation, as Du Bois later termed it[51]—of which Emma Crawford was a part. Black churches and schools, which had grown in number and sophistication over the decades of the late nineteenth century, were both the racial infrastructure and the armor that protected families and communities from the assaults of a hostile wider society. Within these institutions Black Americans could exercise a voice, control their own properties and finances, and achieve recognition for leadership.[52] This framework was fortified by newspapers, magazines, fraternities, sororities, and social organizations that forged national connections, reinforced norms, and facilitated the sharing of information and values.

Emma was connected to these changes in several ways, of which two were especially important: by living in the historic Black village that neighbored Lincoln University, the country's first institution for Black higher education; and through her older brother Merris, a musician who traveled with minstrel shows. The physical proximity of the University was a constant reminder of the social and educational aspirations it represented. Attending its concerts and other activities that were open to villagers additionally exposed Emma to these values—as well as to ambitious young male students from the United States, the Caribbean, and Africa. Eventually, she married one of them, which cemented her ties with both the school and the principles of Black education and middle-class respectability that it espoused. Meanwhile, through her older brother's postcards and letters, Emma was exposed to the ways of a wider world beyond the confines of Chester County and to the understanding that Black people could be active parts of that world.

Lincoln University was just one of a growing number of Black colleges and universities that fostered the emerging middle class. In 1863 there were no southern institutions for the higher and secondary education of Black students.[53] By 1910 there were more than eighty such institutions in northern and southern states. From an initial focus immediately after Emancipation on providing elementary and secondary instruction to the freed slaves, by the early 1900s these schools had begun offering courses and programs at the postsecondary level, including specializations in theology, law, medicine, dentistry, and pharmacy.[54] The first Black fraternities and sororities, beginning with Sigma Pi Phi fraternity, were founded in Philadelphia in 1904. These "Black Greek" intercollegiate organizations—which today number more than twenty—created intergenerational national networks that reinforced the value of education, class-related social norms, public service, and civil rights.

The Black Church also grew rapidly in the early twentieth century, sustaining a surge that had begun during Reconstruction. Baptist churches, which newly freed people could form of their own accord and govern independently, predominated among the new congregations. Meanwhile, the African Methodist Episcopal and African Methodist Episcopal Zion denominations, founded by northern free Black communities in 1816 and 1821 respectively, expanded beyond their original bases through missionary work among former slaves.

Then as now, Black churches were central sources of community organization and resilience, especially considering the virtual absence of social welfare institutions in many southern communities and the frequent exclusion of Black children and families from those that existed. In an 1898 survey, Du Bois documented that Black churches hosted literary and missionary societies, conducted outreach in slums and jails, and sponsored orphanages and homes for the aged, in addition to their religious activities. Urgent social needs were also met by progressive organizations like the National Association of Colored Women, founded in 1895, which organized kindergartens, nursery schools, and day care centers.[55] Meanwhile, organizations like the Odd Fellows, Masons, and Knights of Pythias (not directly affiliated with white organizations with the same names) provided financial assistance when members were in need and helped members' widows and orphans.[56] All of these organizations—and others—were reflective of the focus within northern and southern Black communities on self-help, network development, and collaborative activity.

As Black Americans emerged from the shadow of the plantation, their cultural forms and contributions became more complex. With rising levels of education and income came increasing numbers of artists, writers, and academics, whose exploration and interpretation of the Black experience provided what Deborah Willis terms "subversive resistance," by offering an "other" view of Black identity.[57] Richly varied musical forms, many of which ultimately shaped national and international artistic trends (see chapter 5), fueled every kind of Black religious and secular event.

Emma Crawford and other young Black girls who came of age in the first decade of the new century perhaps had a heady sense of doors opening for them that had been closed to earlier generations. Ties of religion and family provided stability and shared meaning. Education and respectability guided the way forward. Yet they would be keenly aware that their options were sharply limited by both race and gender. Emma's experiences as a young woman are an illuminating navigation of this dynamic period, as both personal narrative and representative of other Black girls' lives.

Cotton Picking Time, Southern Pines, N.C. Postcard Publisher: F.C. Eddy, Southern Pines, N.C.

Chapter Three

Fighting for Their Daily Bread

Imagine being a young woman on the cusp of womanhood in the first decade of the twentieth century. If you were white, it was relatively unlikely that you would expect to work outside of the home—in 1914 about 16 percent of white women were in the workforce. But it was a very different picture for Black women, for whom work had been a necessity since Emancipation and for the preceding generations of enslavement.[1] "A larger proportion of women pursued gainful occupations among negroes than in any other class of the population," it was reported in 1895.[2] This was still true in the first decades of the 1900s, when about 40 percent of Black women were employed, compared to white women's 16 percent.[3] In 1914 Du Bois observed:

That the Negro woman is compelled in so many cases to help in the support of the family, is a fact often overlooked by the casual observer of Negro
life. In 1900 there were 1,832,318 Negro homes in this country. Out of these
walked daily one and one-third million women and girls over ten years of age
to work—four out of every ten as against one out of each six white women.
These then were a group of workers fighting for their daily bread like men,
independent, approaching economic freedom. They furnished a half million
farm laborers, 70,000 farmers, 15,000 teachers and professional folk, 700,000
servants and washerwomen, and 40,000 in trades and merchandising.[4]

In cities, as Du Bois noted, Black women were beginning to branch out into education and commercial enterprises, but for a small-town northern girl like Emma Crawford, options were finite—and generally limited to domestic work. (At one end of the range of possibilities was Emma's relative Abbie Cummings, who was a highly sought-after dressmaker for well-off white women; at the other end was her aunt Sarah, who read tea leaves.) From 1907 to 1910, Emma was employed in domestic service in Chester County, Pennsylvania, and in Princeton, New Jersey. It is certain that this work was not what she preferred to do after completing secondary school, but she faced the reality of needing a job, being Black and female, and living in a rural area that presented few other alternatives. Agricultural work at one of the local farms or dairies, although hypothetically an option, would have been out of the question to her family. Instead, by entering domestic service, Emma was following in the footsteps of her mother, Isabella Ford Crawford—literally so, since they worked for many of the same families, sometimes at the same time.

Emma's experience was typical for northern Black workers, who, both male and female, were largely restricted to employment as laborers and servants (75 percent of Philadelphia's Black workforce was so employed at the end of the nineteenth century).[5] As work went, these jobs were preferable to the backbreaking agricultural peonage depicted in the post-card "Cotton Picking Time," but relative to the options available to white workers in expanding northern economies, they were limited and dead-end. Domestic pay was low, and Black workers were at the bottom of the pay scale. In 1899 average weekly wages in Philadelphia ranged from $2.00 for errand girls to about $4.00 for cooks and laundresses, the best-paid in the hierarchy of Black domestic laborers. Even at the high end of the scale, these earnings were less than half the estimated average weekly wage of $9.40 for all non-farm workers during this period.[6] To make matters worse, even in these low-paying positions, Black workers faced fierce competition from—and lost ground to—newly arrived European immigrants.

Like many Black domestic workers, Emma lived in with her employers, a practice that gradually became less common in the first decades of the twentieth century. Especially in cities, where the rise of apartment living and the introduction of electricity-based home technology decreased the need for live-in staff, daywork became the norm.[7] The work Emma did was labor-intensive and time-consuming. As one of the former domestic workers interviewed by Elizabeth Clark-Lewis reported, "When you live-in, you must do everything but chew they food. Do this, do that, run here, run there, and when you get through—do this!"[8]

In the early years of the century, some households had running water, but many rural families and city dwellers did not. Less affluent people still heated their water on a coal or wood range, rubbed clothes on a wash-board, used hand wringers, and hung clothes on a line to dry. Ever-present soot from fireplaces and wood stoves made it hard to keep homes clean.[9]

Given these conditions, it is no surprise that so many Black women told Isabel Eaton, a researcher who worked with Du Bois, that they wanted to leave domestic service. Specifically, they wanted to escape its overtones of slavery and to better their social standing and wages by becoming teachers or dressmakers.[10] The nontrivial risks of physical and sexual harassment in households that included white men and boys were also a concern.

But finding work outside domestic service was very difficult. "[Black women's] field for exercising their talent and ambition is, broadly speaking, confined to the dining room, kitchen and street," Eaton wrote. In other words, in addition to sex work ("the street"), Black women were confined to cooking, washing and ironing, tending furnaces, cleaning up, and taking care of children. In Philadelphia, other big cities, and wealthier rural households, families typically employed more than one domestic servant, but in many cases, one woman, working in isolation, was responsible for all of these backbreaking chores.

When she completed her education around age seventeen (1906), Emma would have had a clear-eyed sense of her very limited options. The fact that she attended secondary school was a telling sign of the family's values, in a period when even white secondary school graduates were a rarity.[11] A focus on education had consistently helped the Crawfords survive many decades of restricted social opportunities (see chapter 6). Available evidence suggests that a white Quaker couple with deep local roots ran the "colored school" Emma attended, with the assistance of a few Black teachers. The curriculum included, among other topics, English history, botany, zoology, drawing, and music. Emma pressed and labeled plants and kept a music notebook that included transcribed popular songs of the day, such as "Mount Vernon Bells," "Sweet Be Thy Slumbers," and "The Lark." The only material with any racial associations was the song "Old Black Joe," which she wrote as "Old—— Joe," deleting the then-offensive term "Black."

A visit to the Philadelphia Zoo, perhaps in connection with her schoolwork, was referenced in a card from her cousin Anna Ford. The Victorian gatehouses shown on the card are still standing and were designed by Frank Furness and George Hewitt in 1875.[12]

The school's curriculum was unrelated to the jobs its students were likely to fill, but it ably reflected the aspirational "uplift" orientation of the times. The preparation it gave Emma may also have made her more attractive to her employers, who would perhaps have seen her as someone they would not mind having around their children—and an appropriate successor to her equally educated mother. If her employers thought about it at all, they probably viewed domestic work as the natural setting for Black women, even those who had enough education for more-challenging occupations.[13]

One of the oldest postcards in Emma's collection encouraged her to continue her education. "I hope you are getting along nicely in your studies," James W. B. wrote in early 1907. "Remember me to Coal and the family."

Designed by Richard Outcault, the 1902 creator of the comic strip characters Buster Brown, Mary Jane, and Tige, the card depicts three "doctors" preparing to operate on a terrified patient, under the watchful

Entrance Zoological Gardens, Philadelphia, Pa.

"Dear: Didn't we have a lovely time at the Zoo. Sunday. I received your card. Mr. Watkins went upon that train did you see him. Anna"

Mailed in November 1906 to Emma at home. Postcard Publisher: The Metropolitan News Co., Boston.

eye of a stereotypically large and glowering Mammy. Chloroform, kitchen knives, and heavy implements—a hatchet, saw, and wrench—constitute the doctors' medical paraphernalia. The card's humor derives from the clownish fear of the patient and the ridiculously inappropriate tools the doctors are prepared to use on him.

To our eyes, the card's racist imagery is offensive and conflicts with James W. B.'s friendly greeting, but perhaps he'd become inured to the era's commonplace racism.[14] However, it is the only card of its type in Emma's collection, which suggests that she had a different reaction. Perhaps she told her friends not to send her cards of this type—or maybe she destroyed any others she received!—thus deliberately avoiding the racism of the day, just as she refused to write "Old Black Joe" in her school notebook.

The contrast between "Darktown Doctors" and a card Emma received later that year from her older brother Merris (Mike) is instructive. At the time, she and her mother were both working for and living with the Milton Pyle family in West Grove, Pennsylvania, while Merris, a professional musician, was en route from the Appalachian town of Montgomery, West Virginia, to Jackson, Ohio, east of Cincinnati. The

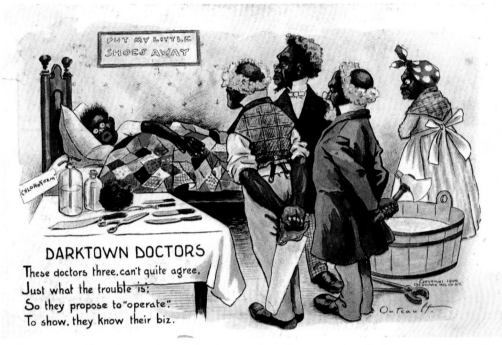

Darktown Doctors. These doctors, three, can't quite agree, Just what the trouble is; So they propose to "operate," To show, they know their biz.

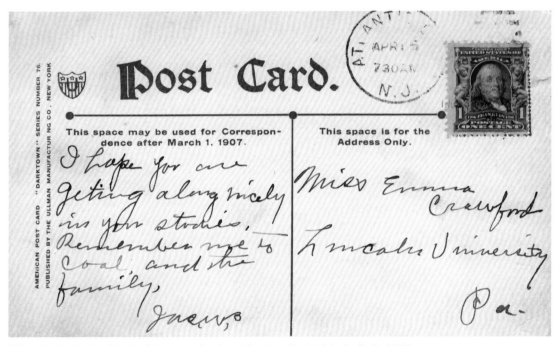

"I hope you are getting along nicely in your studies. Remember me to Coal and the family. Jas. W. B."

Mailed in April 1907 to Emma at home. Postcard Publisher: The Ullman Mfg Co, NY, 1906. The card was one of several in Outcault's "Darktown" series.

"Jackson Ohio, May – 6, By – By

Yours truly Mike"

Mailed on April 30, 1907, to Emma, who was living with the Milton C. Pyle family in West Grove. Postcard Publisher: Philadelphia Post Card Co., Series 6523.

rosy-cheeked "Dutch" girls depicted on his card are a stark departure from the Darktown Doctors. Happily and innocently enjoying a beverage, their pretty, smiling faces invite us to share in their pleasure. In contrast, the doctors' young patient is so frightened that his hair is standing on end, and both his fear and the unsympathetic attitude of his onlookers are a subject of humor. The difference in the cards is just one small reflection of "the massive propaganda campaign demeaning African Americans" that was fundamental to reinforcing early twentieth-century Jim Crow.[15]

It's worth noting that, lacking positive Black images, children identified with these European pictures. Thus, Emma's young cousin Percy Ford equated himself with the young Dutch girl on the card he sent her, writing, "Come along Emma I won't let the ducks harm you let us hurry to the church with these flowers from Percy J Ford." (His added note, "This is my writing," may refer only to the signature, since Percy was younger than ten years old at the time.)

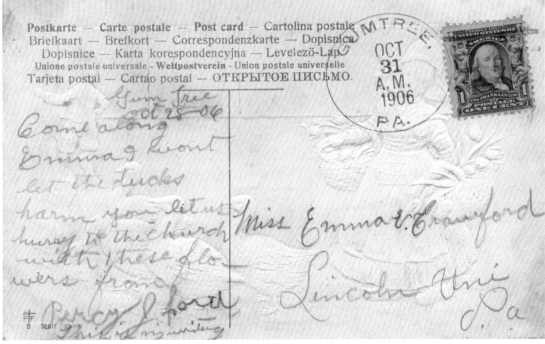

"Gum Tree [Pennsylvania]. Come along Emma, I won't let the ducks harm you. Let us hurry to the church with these flowers from Percy J. Ford. This is my writing."

Mailed on October 31, 1906, to Emma at home. Postcard Publisher: PFB Series 3939.

The Round of Work, 1907–10

In 1907 Emma held the first domestic position that took her away from home for a sustained period. Her parents, who were in their late fifties, were also employed but living apart. Her three older brothers had left the house already, Merris as a professional musician (see chapter 5), William to live with their father and attend school, and Philip to work locally. Staying at home with her mother and not working was simply not an option economically. Moreover, during those times when her mother was away, living at employers' houses, she would have been at home by herself, which was undesirable.

Her friends were also mobile during this period. Like herself, the girls with whom she had gone to school were in domestic service. The boys of her acquaintance, many of whom were students at nearby Lincoln University, worked service jobs over the summer, often at hotels in Atlantic City. Meanwhile, her mother was also employed with local families. In an era when just 5 percent of households had telephones, the constant flow of postcards kept them all efficiently and inexpensively in touch.

To protect their earnings, domestic workers were best off either living at home; being married to, or living with, another wage earner; or living at their place of work. In Isabel Eaton's 1899 survey of Black domestic workers in Philadelphia, most (60 percent) of the single girls lived where they were employed.[16] For many years, Emma did so as well, repeatedly cycling between her employers' homes in the small towns of Chester County and central New Jersey and her own home outside Lincoln University. Like the workers in Eaton's study, she used her wages to help support her mother and other family members.

Depending on the household, her duties were childcare and, sometimes, cooking. The families were generally well-established business owners who could afford domestic servants. Many were members of Pennsylvania's Quaker gentry, whose families traced their roots to colonial Pennsylvania, as Emma's did as well. Several of the families were associated specifically with the New Garden Friends Meeting, located in Toughkenamon, Emma's birthplace.[17]

The family's association with the Quaker community is worth noting, as it was long-standing and perhaps protective, both socially and economically. The first Quaker to settle in what is now known as Pennsylvania was probably Robert Wade, who had emigrated from England in 1675. By 1683 Quaker men and women were meeting monthly in Chester County and other locations. In early Pennsylvania, "Quakers controlled the government, they were the leaders in business and the Friends' meetings had a dominating influence in the communities which sprang up."[18]

The Quakers were early opponents of slavery, which they considered to be incompatible with moral and natural law, and "by 1780 all Quakers in good standing had released their slaves."[19] In the antebellum era, some Quakers participated in loosely organized Underground Railroad networks, while a few made the Underground Railroad their life's work or participated in the organized antislavery movement. One author's judgment is that "any fugitive who had crossed the Mason-Dixon Line and appealed to a Quaker for assistance was either aided or directed to someone who could supply that assistance."[20] By the early twentieth century, the Quakers in Chester County were well established, prosperous, and the inheritors of this tradition of racial liberalism.

For many years Emma's mother, Isabella, worked for the Bushongs, one of the established Quaker families. Emma's brother Philip was named Philip Bushong Crawford in their honor. Another of Emma's brothers, William Fulton Crawford, was named for the Quaker doctor who delivered him. These Black and white families with long roots in Pennsylvania may have felt a kind of mutual allegiance in the face of the nineteenth- and early twentieth-century influx into the state of Irish, Germans, other Europeans, and Black migrants from the South. The European immigrants who flowed into Pennsylvania during Emma's young adulthood were mainly unskilled workers and peasants who strongly challenged Black workers for semiskilled and unskilled jobs.[21] In that respect working with Quaker families may have provided some insulation for the Crawfords from a changing social environment that otherwise powerfully threatened the already-precarious social and economic position of Black Pennsylvanians.

Altogether, in the four-year period from 1907 through 1910, Emma worked for six families. This working pattern was probably similar to that of thousands of other young Black women. It made it difficult for them to sustain friendships and family life—again underscoring the important connective role played by postcards and other correspondence.

Since many—if not all—of Emma's employers knew one another, they undoubtedly shared information about her availability and household skills. Typically, she spent several months at a single household, returned home for a period, then moved to another household. Over the course of a year, she sometimes returned multiple times to work with a particular family.

Eventually, Emma hoped to attend Mercy Hospital and School for Nurses, in Philadelphia. The twenty-bed facility, which opened in 1907 "with much ceremony and pride," was the city's second Black hospital.[22] Described as "a great sacrifice of time and money, tireless endeavor, vision, planning and determination on the part of a group of Negro men and women," it was established under the aegis of Dr. E. Clarence Howard,

To one I love

Mailed in February 1907 to Emma while she was living with the Milton C. Pyle family in West Grove. Postcard Publisher: B.W. 287, Printed in Germany.

Greetings from West Grove; the Waves
"Emma"

This is a fanciful card that Emma mailed in 1907 to her mother while living with the Milton C. Pyle family in West Grove—which is many miles from the closest beach! Postcard Publisher: Art Series, Pub. By the Rose Company, Philadelphia, PA., No. 910.

THE WAVES

the first Black medical graduate of Harvard University. Clearly, attending such an institution would have been a major step forward for Emma. Ultimately, marriage and motherhood kept her from accomplishing this goal, but the aspiration to become a nurse represented her firm intention to rise above the limited horizons of rural life. In this regard her ambitions mirrored Isabel Eaton's finding that "colored city domestics seek other work . . . from the desire to escape social degradation first, from the desire for greater personal freedom next, and finally from the hope of higher remuneration."[23]

◆ ◆ ◆

Emma's first employer was Milton C. Pyle in West Grove, then a small Chester County town of about nine hundred people. For a brief time in 1907, she and her mother both worked in his household—perhaps while Emma served as her mother's apprentice and was trained in the expectations of domestic work. Milton C. Pyle was vice president and cashier of the National Bank of West Grove, and a member of a well-established Chester County family that descended from Robert Pyle, a Quaker who had emigrated from England in 1683. The family was also associated with the Conard Pyle Company, a horticultural house in West Grove that specialized in rose production.[24] Emma was probably responsible for taking care of Milton and Helen's young daughter, Dorothy, who was born in 1904.

Later in 1907 Emma worked for John N. Remsen, who also lived in West Grove. Remsen owned a country store in West Chester that sold stoves and did pump work, plumbing, and steam fitting. He also sold chickens and other agricultural stock.[25]

While working at the Remsens' household, Emma received a card from her childhood friend Gertrude Hall that gives a sense of the distances Black women traveled for domestic work. Gertrude wrote from Haverhill, Massachusetts, some four hundred miles from Lincoln University village, where she was "still at the same place." Haverhill was a progressive community that was associated historically with the abolitionist movement and Underground Railroad. Gertrude expected to return home in about a month's time. She asked Emma about "grandmother"—Emma's grandmother Maria Ford—with whom Gertrude had previously boarded.

Hannah Duston (1657–1736), depicted on the card, is the first woman honored in the United States with a statue. At forty years old and the mother of nine children, she and her newborn daughter were captured by Native Americans during the Raid on Haverhill in King William's War (1697). Later in her captivity, she and two other English captives were said

Hannah Duston Monument, Haverhill, Massachusetts

"*Dear Emma, I haven't heard from you for a long time. Please write and tell me all about the things that have happened. Where is grandmother? I will be up some time the last of Sept. Still at the same place. Gertrude Hall*"

Mailed in August 1907 to Emma, who was living with the John N. Remsen family in West Grove. Postcard Publisher: S. H. Knox & Co.

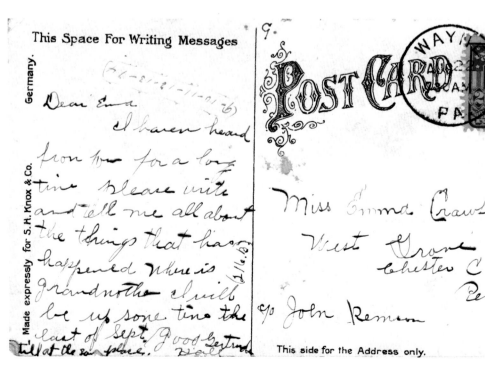

Pine Grove, Pa.

"Dear Emma, I am enjoying myself very much—can't see anything but trees, hills and water. Your mother, Isabella Crawford"

Mailed in 1907 (month obscure) to Emma at home. The postcard publisher is unknown. The dam in the photograph forms Octoraro Lake, in Lancaster County. Octoraro Creek is a 22.1-mile-long tributary of the Susquehanna River.

to have scalped ten of the Native Americans who were holding them hostage. Duston's story became famous more than a hundred years after she died. During the nineteenth century, she was referred to as "a folk hero" and the "mother of the American tradition of scalp hunting."

In Gertrude and Emma's time, a statue with a female subject was very rare. Even today, of the 5,193 public outdoor sculptures of individuals in the United States, less than 8 percent are of women.[26] In honoring Hannah, the statue was also unusual for celebrating an actual woman, rather than one from allegory (e.g., "freedom") or mythology. However, as representative of the vilification of Native Americans and the celebration of westward expansion, the statue has also been contested for decades, leading to recent calls for its removal.[27]

Another card Emma received in 1907, this time from her mother, Isabella, illustrates, like Gertrude's, the distances Black women traveled in connection with work. It was sent from Pine Grove, a small, rural community located among the Appalachian ridges of Eastern Pennsylvania's coal country, about seventy miles from Lincoln University village. The

Best Wishes

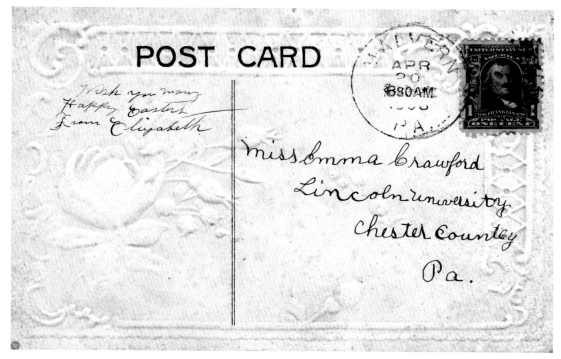

"Wish you many Happy Easters. From Elizabeth"

Mailed on April 20, 1908, to Emma at home. The postcard publisher is unknown.

Wishing you a Happy Christmas
"Hope you may has [sic] *mary* [sic] *Xmas, from Elizabeth"*

Mailed in December 1907 to Emma at home. Postcard Publisher: International Art Publ Co., New York, Series 445. In 1907, postcards had just begun to be popularly used for Christmas greetings. (Ryan, 1982, p. 239)

visit sounds restful—"I can't see anything but trees, hills and water"—but it is doubtful that Isabella was on holiday. It is unclear for whom she was working at the time.

In 1908 Emma worked for a few months for the John Haines family in Malvern, then a small Chester County town of 1,400, now an outer suburb of Philadelphia. Haines, a Quaker, was a coal and lumber merchant. Emma received several holiday postcards from John Haines's daughter-in-law, Elizabeth, which suggests that she had a positive working relationship with the household.

Later in the year, while still working for the Haines family, Emma received a card from her sister-in-law, Edna, who was traveling with Emma's older brother Merris. Sent from Stockton, California, the card

The Hillman Residence, Stockton, Calif.

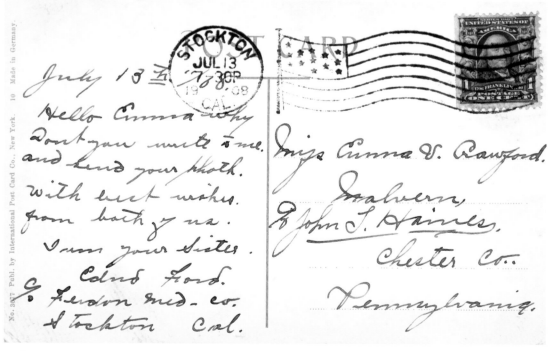

"Hello Emma, why don't you write to me and send your photo. With best wishes from both of us. I am your Sister, Edna Ford. c/o Ferdon Med. Co. Stockton Cal."

Mailed on July 13, 1908, to Emma, who was living with the John Haines family in Malvern, Pennsylvania. Postcard Publisher: International Post Card Co., New York., No. 3077

"Dear Emma, I received your letter and was glad to hear from you. Come over soon and spend the day or afternoon here with me. We all would be very glad to have you come. Your affectionate mother, Isabella Crawford"

Mailed during the summer of 1908 to Emma, who was living with the John Haines family in Malvern, Pennsylvania. The postcard publisher is unknown.

showed the Hillman Residence, built just three years earlier and already recognized as one of the city's most beautiful houses.[28] Merris had been in California since the fall of 1907. In July, when this card was sent, he was working for a medical huckster, "the Great Fer-Don," who dubbed his enterprise the Ferdon Medical Company. It was customary for medicine shows like Fer-Don's to use musicians and minstrels to draw a crowd (see chapter 5). Edna's assertion "I am your Sister" demonstrates how family ties were reinforced across the miles.

While Emma was employed by the Haines family, Isabella asked her to visit—whether at her own Lincoln University home or at an employer's home is unclear. As with the card her mother had sent from Pine Grove, the message is warm yet rather formal to modern ears, veiling the closeness of their relationship: *I received your letter and was glad to hear from you. Come over soon and spend the day or afternoon here with me. We all would be very glad to have you come. Your affectionate mother, Isabella Crawford.*

Later in 1908 Emma worked for the Chandler family in Kennett Square, a town then numbering about 1,600 people. Isaac Eugene Chandler, a Quaker, was "the well known proprietor of an extensive and well appointed pharmacy at Kennett Square, [and] a man of great enterprise, good business qualifications, undaunted perseverance and the utmost integrity." The son of one of Chester County's "leading merchants"—whose Broad Street house is now a Kennett Square landmark—Chandler and his wife, Nettie, had a son, S. Walter, who was ten or eleven years old when Emma worked for the family.[29]

While living with the Chandlers, Emma received several cards more from Edna (or Essie) and Merris (also see chapter 5). One warmly affectionate message, sent from Berkeley, California, directly addresses the importance of letters and cards for maintaining the closeness of relationships in the face of months of separation.

Like Merris's card, many in Emma's collection reference the importance of letters, cards, and personal visits for maintaining relationships in a world where telephones were not commonplace. For example, a 1908 holiday card from her cousin Anna, who was a dressmaker in Media, urges Emma to visit, and to bring along her close friend Helen, with whom she had a sisterly relationship.

Emma spent at least part of the 1908 Christmas season working for the Chandler family, where she received a card from her mother—perhaps hand delivered rather than mailed.

In 1909 Emma continued to work intermittently for the Chandlers and lived at home when she was not employed. Early in the year, while she was living with the Chandlers, her friend Retha Coates wrote from Philadelphia to ask how she had spent the holidays. Her message gives a sense of

4166 Berkeley, Cal., North Hall, University of California

Berkeley, Cal., North Hall, University of California

"Dear Sister, You say I don't send cards, when have you sent any? Essie says write to her, she is here with me. Write soon from your loving Brother, M. P. F. c/o Fer-don Med. Co. Berkeley, Cal."

Mailed on December 5, 1908, to Emma, who was living with the Isaac E. Chandler family in Kennett Square, Pennsylvania. Postcard Publisher: Paul C. Koeber Co., New York City and Kirchheim, No. 4166. North Hall, which was erected in 1873 and razed in 1917, was part of the original nucleus of the UC-Berkeley campus. Berkeley School of Information. (n.d.). *About South Hall*. Retrieved April 14, 2018, from https://www.ischool.berkeley.edu/about/southhall.

A Joyful Christmas

"200 N. Plum St. Media Pa. Hello Emma, How is Lincoln? Why don't you write or come see us some time. You and Helen come during the holidays or some Saturday. Merry Xmas, Anna F."

Mailed on December 23, 1908, to Emma at home. Postcard Publisher: The Rose Company, XMAS-Dogs series, 1907

"From your mother, wish you much happiness."

Delivered in December 1908 to Emma, who was living with the Isaac E. Chandler family in Kennett Square, Pennsylvania.

POST CARD.

THIS SIDE FOR CORRESPONDENCE.

THE ADDRESS TO BE WRITTEN ON THIS SIDE.

PLACE POSTAGE STAMP HERE

DOMESTIC ONE CENT

FOREIGN TWO CENTS

PRINTED IN GERMANY

*From Your
Mother
Wish you much
happiness.*

*Miss Emma Crawford
C/o Eugene Chandler,
Kennett Square,
Penna.*

"Hello Emma. How did you spend Xmas and the holidays? Helen & I have just tried to see how much we could go. Wish you were here. Retha Coates"

Mailed in January 1909 to Emma and addressed to both her home address and an unspecified address in Kennett Square. The postcard publisher is unknown.

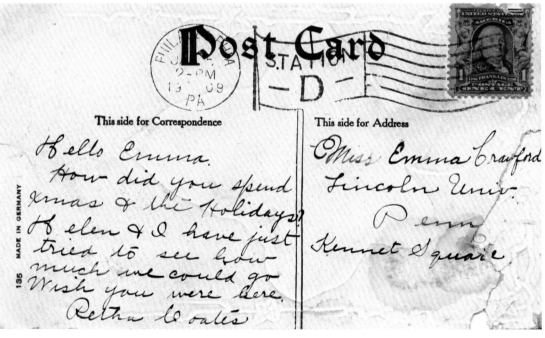

how young working women valued, and took advantage of, their vacation time: "Helen [Wesley] and I have just tried to see how much we could go."

A warm Valentine's Day card from her cousin Anna, sent to Emma at the Chandlers, perhaps relieved some of the loneliness of spending long stretches of time working in isolation and away from her friends and family members.

In the spring of 1909, Emma's friend Helen wrote from Philadelphia, where she was still working, and chided her for being out of touch. Emma was continuing with the Chandlers.

Late in 1909 Emma changed employers for the fifth time in three years and began to work for the Joseph Wilson Howe family. Her position with them continued into the following year, with the 1910 census listing both Emma and her friend Helen Wesley as residents of their home at 318 Harvard Avenue in Swarthmore.

The Howe family was socially more prominent than the households that had employed Emma before and, as such, represented a kind of promotion. This suggests that the impermanence of her previous positions was most likely a typical experience in domestic service, not a negative reflection on the quality of her work. In fact, the contemporary view that "if you get a good class of colored people they are the most faithful, honest, and biddable servants in the world" would have worked to Emma's advantage, given her upbringing and education.[30]

But if working with a wealthier, higher-profile family was an upward move for Emma, her responsibilities—childcare—were the same. From one placement to the next, there was little variance in her duties, and on the job she had few if any chances to acquire new skills. Her experience in this regard comported with broader contemporary observations about the dead-end nature of domestic service and the need for it to be considered a profession, with opportunities for training.[31]

Working for the Howes exposed Emma to levels of wealth and prestige that were a step above her previous experiences among Chester County's Quaker gentry. It is unclear how Emma was referred to the family. Unlike most of her previous employers, they were not Quakers but Presbyterians with southern roots. However, one of the faculty members at Lincoln University, which was affiliated with the Presbyterian Church, may have made the connection.

The Howe family lived first in Primos, now part of Upper Darby Township near West Philadelphia, then in Swarthmore. Joseph Wilson Howe, called J. Wilson, was the nephew of US president-to-be Woodrow Wilson and head clerk at the Philadelphia Railroad Company. His wife, Virginia Peyton Knight Howe, was a well-known southern socialite, "declared to

To my Valentine

"Dear, Accept my love. Will write soon, your cousin A. M. Ford."

Mailed on February 15, 1909, to Emma, who was living with the Isaac E. Chandler family in Kennett Square, Pennsylvania.
Postcard Publisher: A & S

"Hello Emma, Got home all right. Where have you been? Why don't you write? Helen"

Mailed on May 18, 1909, to Emma, who was living with the Isaac E. Chandler family in Kennett Square, Pennsylvania. Postcard Publisher: ASB 339.

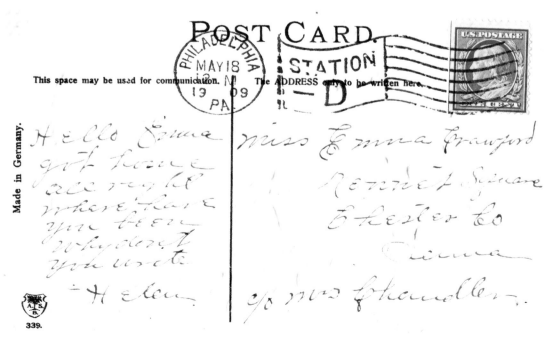

Colored photographic postcard of Joseph Wilson Howe, Jr., circa 1910.

be one of the most beautiful women [in Virginia]."[32] Their son, Joseph Wilson Howe Jr., was five years old when Emma lived with the family.

Virginia and J. Wilson Howe's marriage was tumultuous. Five years earlier, in 1904, Virginia had divorced J. Wilson with the intention of marrying Justin Perceval, her childhood sweetheart—whom she then deserted at the altar. While divorced, Virginia supported herself as a writer for one of the Charlottesville, Virginia, newspapers, covering social items as "Fluffy." She was "known throughout the South as a writer of considerable ability." Presumably, her beauty and family protected her from the social disfavor of being a divorced woman with a small child. Sometime between 1907 and when Emma started working for them, the Howes remarried.[33]

In this photographic postcard, Joseph Wilson Howe Jr. is wearing a version of the then-fashionable tunic suit, similar to a Buster Brown suit. It was still common to outfit boys in dresses at the turn of the century, but by the 1910s it was becoming less so. A few years later, J. Wilson Jr., "namesake of the President's father, . . . had the honor of eating the first viands served in the white House during the Wilson administration. His crowning ambition is to be a cowboy in the wild and wooly west."[34]

Many years later, in 1928, Virginia Howe's drowned corpse was found beneath a railroad trestle in Virginia Beach, Virginia. It was undetermined at the time whether she had jumped or had fallen.[35]

"Dear Sister: How are you and Helen? Hope you folks keep well, we are having beautiful weather now and it is so very prety [sic] out here just now would love for you to come out—From Sister Eva"

Mailed in April 1910 to Emma, who was living with the J. Wilson Howe family in Swarthmore, Pennsylvania. The postcard publisher is unknown.

While working for the Howes, Emma received a card from her coworker Helen Wesley's younger sister Eva that, like the card from her sister-in-law Edna, emphasized their relationship as "sisters." "Dear Sister," Eva wrote, signing herself "Sister Eva."

Fictive kin—or individuals who are unrelated by either blood or marriage but regard one another in kinship terms—are important members of the informal networks of African American families.[36] For Eva and Emma, fictive sisterhood translated into a lifelong relationship.

In this period Emma was mailed several sexist cards. Like "Darktown Darkies," these cards derived their humor from the presumed ineptness and/or unattractiveness of their subjects—in this case single women without male companions. Since the cards remained in Emma's collection, perhaps their imagery did not bother her as much as racism did.

Although the women were not explicitly identified as suffragettes, the cards echo those of the period that mocked women's demand for the vote.[37] One of the cards depicted a ghoul-like woman and referenced temperance, by 1909 a mass movement that resulted in the Eighteenth Amendment to the United States Constitution in 1919, which outlawed the production and sale of alcohol (Prohibition).

In the fall of 1910, Emma relocated from Swarthmore to the household of J. Wilson Howe's uncle, Woodrow Wilson, then the thirteenth president of Princeton University. Helen Wesley accompanied Emma to Princeton, where Emma finally graduated from the familiar role of providing childcare to working as an apprentice chef. The position was initially promising: in August, Emma sent her mother a postcard of Prospect, then the presidential residence, with a cheery note: "This is the house where we are working. I guess you can imagine how large it is, From Emma." Her mother was living at Bloomfield, the historic home of the Chambers family in Kennett Square. She was then in her early sixties, reflecting the ongoing need for income.

Although Emma's responsibilities in the Woodrow Wilson household were a promotion from childcare, it was not a happy situation. In a foretaste of the racist attitudes for which Wilson's presidential administration became known, his three daughters—Margaret, Eleanor, and Jessie—went out of their way to make life difficult for Helen and Emma. Their many pranks included intercepting and burning the girls' mail—their only means of communicating with the outside world.

Because of the daughters' hostility, Emma did not remain with the Wilson household when he was elected governor of New Jersey in November 1910. We can assume that her sense of integrity outweighed whatever benefits might have come from staying with the family. Her departure was troubled and premature, but she has a lasting footprint at Princeton

Such Taste! (In the mouth)

Mailed in 1910 to Emma, who was living with the J. Wilson Howe family in Swarthmore, Pennsylvania. The postcard publisher is unknown.

Such Taste! (In the mouth)

A Breaker of few Hearts but of much Crockery

A Breaker of few Hearts but of much Crockery

An unmailed card. The postcard publisher is unknown.

"Lips that Touch Liquor Shall Never Touch Mine"

An unmailed card. The postcard publisher is unknown.

Prospect, President's Residence, Princeton University, Princeton, N.J.

"This is the house where we are working. I guess you can imagine how large it is. From Emma"

Mailed in August 1910 to Isabella Crawford, who was living with the Chambers family in Kennett Square. Postcard Publisher: Detroit Photographic Co., 1903

in a brick placed by her great-granddaughter, the writer and artist Lex Brown, in 2012.

Two years after Emma left Princeton, Woodrow Wilson was elected the twenty-eighth president of the United States. Wilson is lauded for his contributions to liberal reforms at home and his fight for the extension of democratic liberties and human rights abroad, but he was a southerner, and his administration also introduced an enduring, regressive racial legacy.[38]

Before Wilson's election, the question of his racial attitudes had generated guarded optimism from Du Bois, who commented that "on the whole, we do not believe that Woodrow Wilson admires Negroes . . . [but] we have . . . a conviction that Mr. Wilson will treat Black men and their interests with farsighted fairness."[39] However, within months of Wilson's taking office, Du Bois's optimism was defeated by the administration's institution of government-wide segregation of workplaces, restrooms, and lunchrooms. "Black Republican appointees in the South were discharged and replaced by whites, and government workers in Washington who had worked side by side for years found themselves separated by race."[40]

"Alexis Brown '12 in commemoration of Emma Crawford Skerrett"

In response, Du Bois urged Wilson to support equal rights, publicly imploring in his *Open Letter to Woodrow Wilson* that he hold true to the highest principles of American democracy: "We want to be treated as men. We want to vote. We want our children educated. We want lynching stopped. We want no longer to be herded as cattle on street cars and railroads. We want the right to earn a living, to own our own property and to spend our income unhindered and uncursed."[41]

Wilson quickly disappointed any hopes that he would support the civil rights of African Americans. Ultimately, his administration brought to power a generation of political leaders from the Old South who would play influential, racially oppressive roles in Washington for generations to come.

Woodrow Wilson was Emma's last long-term employer before she married, her experience with his abusive daughters bringing her working years to a jarring conclusion. It was a matter of enduring pride in the family that with motherhood she was able to stop working outside the home. Maintaining a stable family life under the conditions of her on-again, off-again employment would have been exceedingly difficult—although this was the reality for thousands of Black women, including her own mother. Working also interfered with romance and friendships, but youthful energy—and postcards—found a way across that hurdle.

Chapter Four

Romance and Friendship

Advice to Girls
Frances Ellen Watkins Harper

Nay, do not blush! I only heard
You had a mind to marry;
I thought I'd speak a friendly word, So just one moment tarry.

Wed not a man whose merit lies
In things of outward show,
In raven hair or flashing eyes,
That please your fancy so.

But marry one who's good and kind,
And free from all pretence;
Who, if without a gifted mind,
At least has common sense.[1]

Francis E. W. Harper's 1868 advice for young African American women was an expression of mid-nineteenth-century romantic ideals that could be far removed from reality. In the years immediately after the Civil War especially, Black family life was in recovery from the shattering legacy of centuries of slavery, during which economic considerations thoroughly violated the integrity and agency of Black households: marriages were not legally recognized, families were ripped apart on the auction block, and whites had unfettered sexual access to Black men, women, and children. Remarkably, despite this history, by 1890—a mere generation after Emancipation—Black men and women had nearly the same rate of marriage as whites.[2] A persistent difference, however, was that Black women were more likely than white women to divorce their partners.[3] Viewing Black divorce rates through mid-Victorian eyes, Du Bois attributed them to "lax moral habits" that were left over from slavery, but he also recognized that economic difficulties placed profound strains on Black marriages. Postponement of marriage among the young—"of those in the twenties over 40 per cent are still unmarried, and of those in the thirties 21 per cent"—contributed to what he perceived to be declining morality. "Negro girls no longer marry in their 'teens as their mothers and grandmothers did."[4]

By 1910 marriage rates for Black women had increased compared to twenty years earlier (defeating Du Bois's anxiety) and were just slightly lower than the rate for white women (57 percent compared to 59 percent). Sixteen percent of Black women were widowed or divorced, compared to 11 percent of white women.[5] These numbers suggest that Emma Crawford was about as likely as her white peers to anticipate getting married. She did so at age twenty-four, exemplifying the trend toward later marriage that Du Bois had documented.

Finding prospective mates was not easy for young Black women who, like Emma, were at work most of the week in white households. Du Bois acknowledged the difficulty, commenting that servant girls "form chance acquaintances here and there, thoughtlessly marry and soon find that the husband's income cannot alone support a family." Emma enjoyed the significant advantage granted by living in the village on the perimeter of all-male Lincoln University. Many of her suitors were university students, "talented tenthers" with attractive earning potential and future social standing. Ultimately, a young man who had immigrated from the Caribbean to attend Lincoln University won her hand.

For Emma and her suitors and friends, postcards with preprinted messages were a convenient romantic device, with or without an additional flirtatious message. There are several examples in her collection. One aspiring admirer (with an indecipherable name) borrowed a line from "I'll Be with You When the Roses Bloom Again," a still-popular song, originally released in 1901, about a soldier and his sweetheart.[6]

Meanwhile, in 1908, when she was living with the John Haines household in Malvern, Emma received "Maybe," an ambiguous, and unsigned, romantic appeal.

In the 1908 New Year card that follows, "Silvester" recasts lines from *Anne of Green Gables*, the best seller that was first published earlier that same year. The original lines were: "When twilight drops her curtain down / And pins it with a star / Remember that you have a friend / Though she may wander far."[7]

In July 1909 "H.G.O." sent what was perhaps intended to be a flirtatious card, given its reference to "You're the Queen of Hearts." Someone should have told him that dental work is not a romantic subject!

Just Say You Care

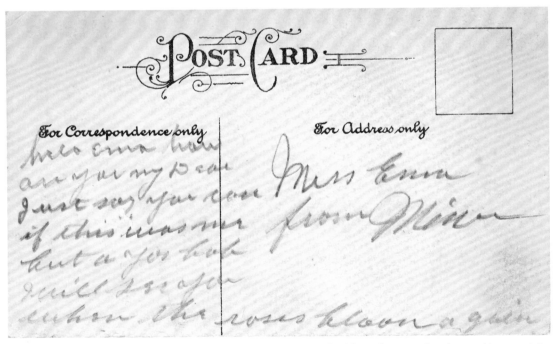

"Helo [sic] *Emma how are you my Dear Just say you care if this was me but [illegible] I will see you when the roses bloom again"*

An unmailed card. The postcard publisher is unknown.

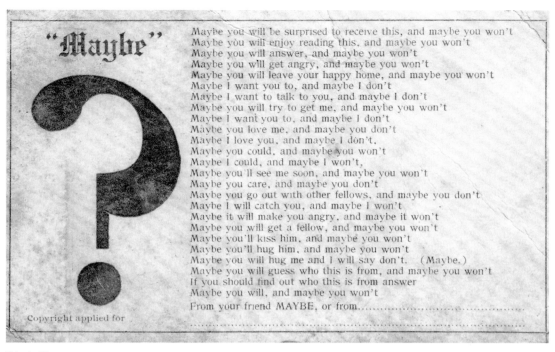

"Maybe"?

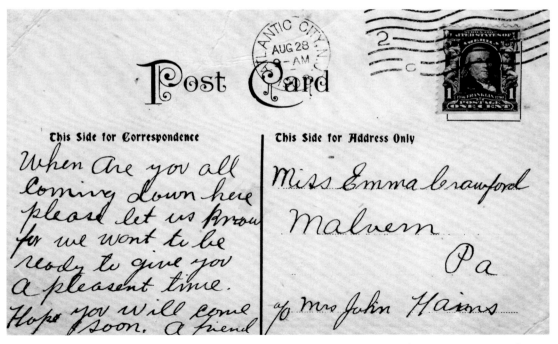

"When are you all coming down here. Please let us know for we want to be ready to give you a pleasant time. Hope you will come soon. A friend"

Mailed on August 28, 1908, to Emma, who was living with the John Haines family in Malvern, Pennsylvania. The postcard publisher is unknown.

Best Wishes for 1909

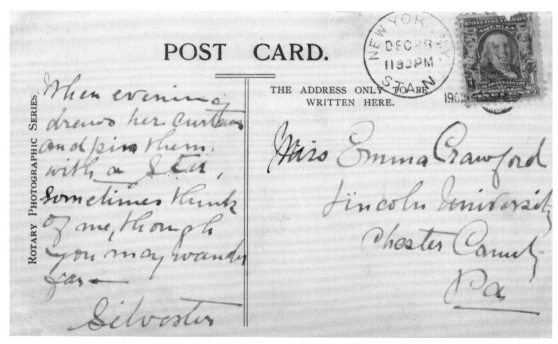

"When evening draws her curtains, and pins them with a star, sometimes think of me, though you may wander far—Silvester"

Mailed on December 28, 1908, to Emma at home. Postcard Publisher: Rotary Photographic Series.

Beguile me not with winsome arts. I have the "0" You're Queen of Hearts.

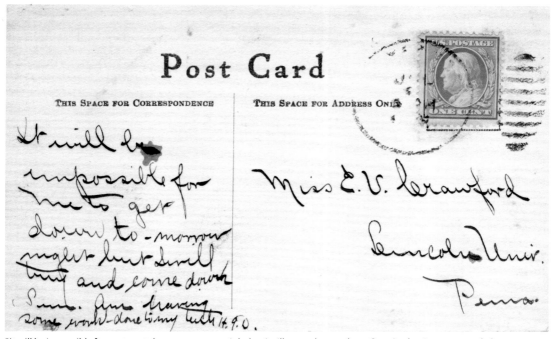

"It will be impossible for me to get down to-morrow night but I will try and come down Sun. Am having some work done to my teeth. H.G.O."

Mailed in July 1909 to Emma at home. Postcard Publisher: E. B. Scofield, 1909.

"Dear Friend, I felt awfully disappointed because you did not come in Sunday night. I waited in the station until 7 o'clock. Many pleasant memories of St. Valentine. Yours truly, Wm. A. Hall"

Mailed on February 14, 1910, to Emma, who was living with the J. Wilson Howe family in Primos, Pennsylvania. The postcard publisher is unknown.

This mask will not hide my love for you;
So take it my Dear, for a Valentine true.

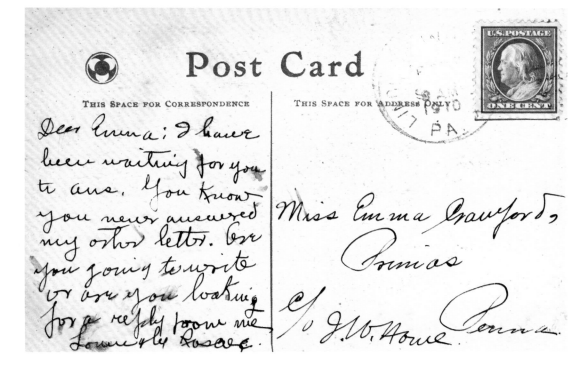

This mask will not hide my love for you,
So take it my Dear, for a Valentine true.

Copyright 1908 by J. Thomas

"*Dear Emma: I have been waiting for you to ans. [answer]. You know you never answered my other letter. Are you going to write or are you looking for a reply from me? Lovingly, Roscoe [?]*"

Mailed in 1910 to Emma, who was living with the J. Wilson Howe family in Primos, Pennsylvania. Postcard Publisher: J. Thomas, 1908.

Post Card

THIS SPACE FOR CORRESPONDENCE

THIS SPACE FOR ADDRESS ONLY

U.S. POSTAGE
ONE CENT

Dear Emma; I have
been waiting for you
to ans. You know
you never answered
my other letter. Are
you going to write
or are you looking
for a reply from me
Lovingly Roscoe.

Miss Emma Crawford,
Primos
C/o J. W. Howe Penna.

In February 1910, Emma received a Valentine from Wm. A. Hall (William Alexander Hall), a theological student at Lincoln University, when she and Helen Wesley were living with the J. Wilson Howe family. Did she stand him up at the station? It appears so. Nevertheless, he seems to have been optimistic about a future relationship.

Another suitor (Roscoe?) also sent a disappointed Valentine's card in 1910, asking Emma why she had not responded to earlier correspondence.

Atlantic City

Several of the young men who pursued Emma wrote her from summer jobs in Atlantic City, then in its heyday as a major vacation resort. As the first urban space in the United States that was devoted primarily to recreation and leisure, Atlantic City offered numerous job opportunities in its many boarding houses, hotels, and restaurants.[8] Black workers were an important part of its image, because "there was no better means to reinforce the illusion of being part of the upper crust than to be doted over by obliging 'colored servants' dressed in uniforms."[9]

In its early years, Atlantic City was integrated, but in the summer of 1904 Black visitors were ordered off the carousels and other boardwalk amusements. Thereafter, white business owners vigilantly enforced an unofficial color line that restricted Black beachgoers to a "colored beach" between Mississippi and Missouri Avenues. Later known as Chicken Bone Beach, the area blossomed over the years into a lively vacation destination for African Americans throughout the Northeast.[10] At the beginning of the twentieth century, an established Black community was also beginning to take shape in the city, called the Northside because it was north of the railroad tracks.

"T.J." sent Emma a picture of the (segregated) Berkshire Inn. Of the more than a thousand Atlantic City hotels, the inn was among those distinguished by having a prestigious boardwalk address.[11]

Emma was living with the Isaac E. Chandler family in Kennett Square in 1909 when she received the following unsigned card from a suitor who was working in Atlantic City and living in the Black Northside.

Emma was at home when she received another unsigned card. As with the previous card, the sender's address placed him in Atlantic City's Black Northside.

Berkshire Inn

Note the crude quality of the drawing in comparison to Emma's German postcards.

"I hope that you are having a nice time. I think of you often. I am having a grand time and wish you could be here. from TJ"

Mailed on March 18 (year unknown) to Emma at home. Postcard Publisher: A. O. Alexander, Advertising, Atlantic City, N.J., number 25878.

"I'm Almost Ready to Believe You."

"I'M ALMOST READY TO BELIEVE YOU."

"115 N. New York Ave., Atlantic City. Dear Emma. This will let you know of my where abouts. I hope to hear from you. Sorry that I did not get to be with you longer the other evening, I had something to tell you. This leaves me well. Sincerely"

Mailed on April 27, 1909, to Emma, who was living with the Isaac E. Chandler family in Kennett Square, Pennsylvania. The postcard publisher is unknown.

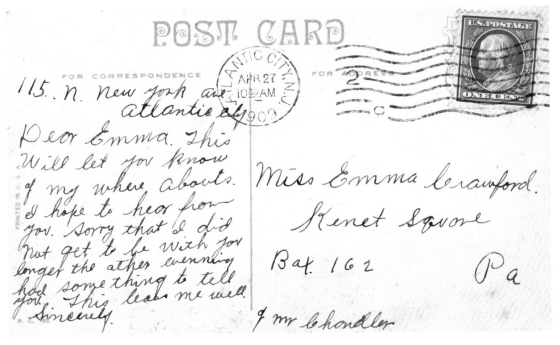

Souvenir from Atlantic City

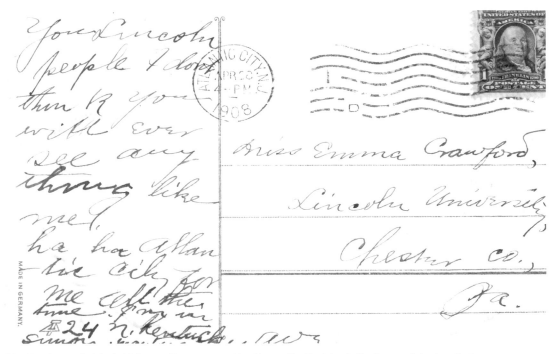

"You Lincoln people, I don't think you will ever see anything like me. Ha, Ha. Atlantic City for me all the time. I'm in 24 N. Kentucky—————"

Mailed on April 28, 1908, to Emma at home. The postcard publisher is unknown.

Unrequited Love

Thomas Casby Boyd was one of the students who wrote Emma from Atlantic City. Boyd graduated from the college at Lincoln University in 1908 and from the Theological Seminary in 1911.[12] On returning to his home state of Arkansas, he became a minister at the Presbyterian Church in the town of Brinkley. His romance with Emma began and ended in 1908, while he was attending the university. One card, sent while he was working in Atlantic City, chided her in its printed message for not keeping in touch: "And if you do as you ought, you will send back a tho't." Boyd's written message suggests unrequited affection, along with the possibility that they would not be reunited: "I shall try and not forget the dream. But it will be a long time before you see me again."

Later that year, he mentioned "another fellow" whom he apparently viewed as a romantic competitor—"I see why you would not have time to see us if we had come by there"—even while affectionately adding "sweet dreams" to the front of the card.

The year 1908 closed with a final card from Thomas to Emma, depicting the Elk Fountain at the reservoir in Reading, Pennsylvania. Thomas said he regretted not having seen her, but he did not express any plans to do so. The relationship (or at least his hope of having one) was seemingly over.

In 1907 and 1908, "Jas. B." was also pursuing Emma. He sent one hopeful card from Atlantic City in 1907 ("Darktown Doctors," chapter 3) and two more in 1908. As his reference to an evening at Mrs. Wesley's house indicates, many of Emma's interactions with young men were in social settings chaperoned by adults, as befitted "respectable" young women.

The courtship seems to have gone poorly, judging from a card Jas. B. sent on April 9 that proclaimed, "Saddest words of tongue or pen are these three words I'm stung again." His message about Helen, Mrs. Wesley's older daughter and Emma's close friend, suggests that the young men and women were part of a friendly circle that was also a socially approved way to meet prospective partners.

On April 13 "Jas." sent a bird's-eye view of Atlantic City, with no accompanying message. Introduced in the 1850s, aerial photography forever changed how humans perceived their environments, and Emma, living in villages and small towns with, at best, two-story structures, would have appreciated the novelty of seeing Atlantic City from a holistic perspective that was possible only from above.[13] At the time, the Inlet was a popular waterfront attraction that included a two-story pavilion that accommodated large fishing and hunting excursions.

❖ ❖ ❖

This card comes to find you and gently remind you of A friend (T. Casby B.) by name—And if you do as you ought, you will send back a tho't, at once, to the same.

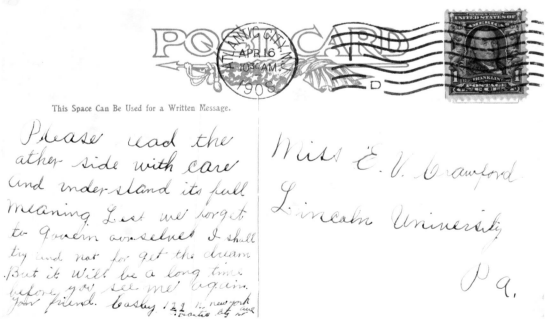

"*Please read the other side with care and understand its full meaning lest we forget to govern ourselves. I shall try and not forget the dream. But it will be a long time before you see me again. Your friend. Casby. 122 N. New York Ave., Atlantic City*"

Mailed on April 16, 1908, to Emma at home. Postcard publisher: Leota Way, Denver, Colo., No. 9, 1907

I am sticking so *close*, I really haven't a minute to spare to write more.

"*We had a jolly time doing the commencement. Would that you all could have been there. I have forgotten your address, but this is as near as I can remember. If you get this answer at once, so I may know. Remember me to Helen. I see why you would not have time to see us if we had come by there. You had another fellow to drive to Wayne. Thomas. 113 N. New York Ave., Atlantic City, N.J.*"

Mailed on June 12, 1908, to Emma, who was living with the John Haines family in Malvern, Pennsylvania. Postcard Publisher: A.Q., Southwick, New York, 1908

Reading, Pa. Drinking Fountain at Reservoir

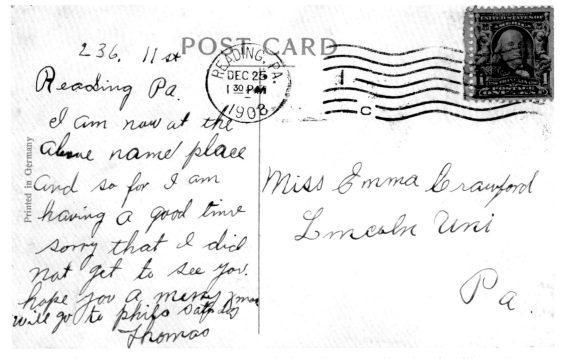

"236 11 St, Reading Pa. I am now at the above named place and so far I am having a good time. Sorry that I did not get to see you. Hope you [have] a merry xmas. Will go to Phila Saturday. Thomas"

Mailed on December 25, 1908, to Emma at home. The postcard publisher is unknown.

This message, dear, I send post haste; It is that I would be with you; And from your lips the nectar taste; Oh birdie, give my message true.

This message, dear, I send post haste,
It is that I would be with you,
And from your lips the nectar taste,
Oh birdie, give my message true.

"I was down to Mrs. Wesley's evenning [sic] thinking that you would be there but fail [sic] to find you. When will you be there? Would like to come down on the evening you are over. May be you will let me know and maybe you won't May be you would like for me to come and may be you won't. Friend JB."

Mailed in 1908 to Emma, who was living with the Isaac E. Chandler family in Kennett Square, Pennsylvania. The postcard publisher is unknown.

Postkarte — Carte postale — Post card — Cartolina postale
Briefkaart — Brefkort — Correspondenzkarte — Dopisnica
Dopisnice — Karta korespondencyjna — Levelező-Lap
Unione postale universale - Weltpostverein - Union postale universelle
Tarjeta postal — Cartáo postal — ОТКРЫТОЕ ПИСЬМО

Miss Emma Crawford

Kennett

Pa

% Mr Eugene Chandler

Saddest words of tongue or pen are these three words I'm stung again.

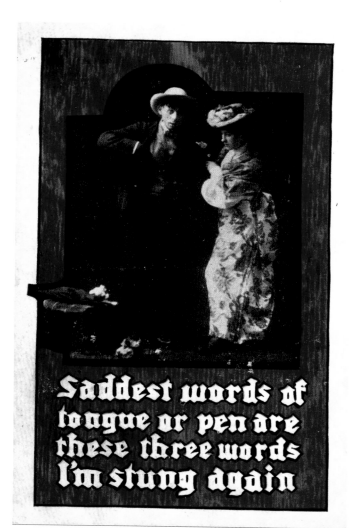

Saddest words of
tongue or pen are
these three words
I'm stung again

"Don't let Helen sleep too much. Keep her awake until I return. Be good. Jas. B."

Mailed on April 9, 1908, to Emma at home. Postcard publisher: Mostwood Series, Pub. By EB&E Co., Detroit

Birds Eye View, Showing Inlet. Atlantic City, N.J.

Mailed on April 13, 1908, to Emma at home. Atlantic City, New Jersey. Postcard publisher: S. Langsdorf & Co., New York, S. 818.

As several of Emma's cards reflect, group activities were an opportunity for socially approved courtship. The following card, from "Glenn" to Emma, mentions in one swoop skating, sleighing, Lincoln University's orchestra, and dancing. It's likely that Glenn was Eugene Herndon Glenn, at the time a baker at Lincoln University and eventually steward of the University's refectory. The University's orchestra was highly regarded: "The singing of Negro melodies and the music of the orchestra of the young men of the university was one of the most attractive features of [an] afternoon," one report noted.[14]

Emma and her peers amused themselves and interacted romantically in ways like those of their white peers—although socially separate from them. Their recreational options were limited, given their race and the rural location, but Du Bois would have found them to be substantially more wholesome than in Philadelphia, where "many of the idlers and rascals of the slums play on the affections of silly servant girls, and either ruin them or lead them into crime, or more often live on a part of their wages."[15]

Dear! Am having a jolly time. Don't Worry!

"We are having a time here now skating and sleighing. The Univ. Orchestra gave a musicale and dance in Westchester last week. I went and we certainly had a sweet time. I wished for you. Remember me to the others. Glenn"

Mailed in December 1910 to Emma, who was living with the Woodrow Wilson family in Princeton, New Jersey. The postcard publisher is unknown.

Friendship and Family Ties

Aside from romance, friendly relationships with relatives and young men and women are well represented in Emma's postcard collection. The exchanges communicate sustained, warm feelings among people who clearly valued friendship and family ties. They convey a sense of people getting on with their lives despite difficult circumstances, for whom the mutual support reflected in their exchanges was undoubtedly sustaining.

For example, in 1906 Eva Wesley sent Emma a quick note, perhaps apologizing for not answering a letter. The card was initially addressed to "Anna"—as though dictated—and was later corrected. It shows the State Normal School, which opened in 1871 and is now known as West Chester University.

Celebrating the arrival of 1907, Emma's cousin Anna Ford simply added her initials to a preprinted New Year card decorated with flowers and a cozy rural cottage.

On a New Year card, received the same day as Anna's, Emma deliberately obscured the message (but preserved the card!).

In April 1907 Emma's older brother William Fulton Crawford sent cards from Ercildoun, Pennsylvania, a small settlement that had been a center of the Underground Railroad in the nineteenth century, and from Coatesville. Coatesville was an early twentieth-century center for steel production, and William was a "laborer" there, according to the 1910 census. Emma was at home in Lincoln University when William wrote her in early April and was working for the Milton Pyle family in West Grove when she received his second card later in the month.

Eva Wesley's card of Fairmount Park arrived during the summer of 1907. Emma was still living with the Pyle family in West Grove. The magnificent park, which now covers nearly ten thousand acres, was already more than a half-century old when Eva visited the city.

Emma was back in Lincoln University when she received an initialed German card of a bucolic springtime scene. "F.G." was presumably the same person as "F.W.G.," who also wrote to her.

In the fall of 1907, a card from Emma's cousin Anna asked when she was coming to Media, about thirty-one miles away and accessible via local railroad. Anna's card was by Raphael Tuck & Sons, one of the most well-known companies in the turn-of-the-century postcard boom. Their reach was global, as reflected in an Irish scene being available for purchase in Chester County. The company was so successful that it "opened up a new field of labor for artists, lithographers, engravers, printers, ink and paste board makers, and several other trade classes."[16]

State Normal School, West Chester Pa.

"Dear Emma—Don't think I am mean for not answering, but will next week if nothing prevents. Sincerely yours, Eva

Mailed on March 30, 1906, to Emma at home. Postcard publisher: Poly-Chrome, no. 6607

A Happy New Year

"A.F."

Mailed on December 27, 1906, to Emma at home.
The postcard publisher is unknown.

Wishing you a happy New Year

Message deliberately obscured.

Mailed on December 27, 1906, to Emma at home. Postcard: B.W. 294

Presbyterian Church. Coatesville, Pa.

Presbyterian Church. Coatesville, Pa.

"I am well hope to hear from you soon I am your BWFC [Brother William Fulton Crawford] Ercildoun, Ches Co, Pa. April 10. 9[?]o7."

Mailed on April 10, 1907, to Emma at home. Postcard publisher: The American News Company, New York, Leipzig, Dresden, A 7178

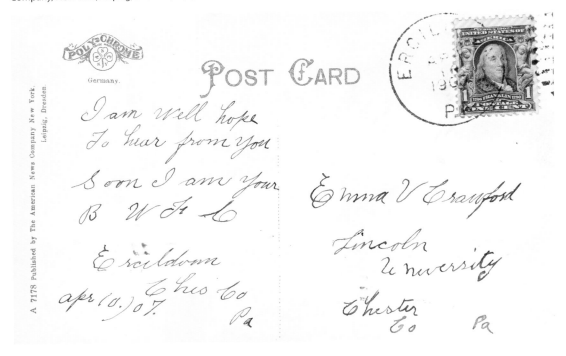

Best Wishes.

"All well. Your B, WFC." [Brother, William Fulton Crawford]

Mailed on April 24, 1907, to Emma, who was living with the Milton C. Pyle family in West Grove, Pennsylvania. Postcard publisher: S. Langsdorf & Co., New York, Germany.

Washington Monument, Fairmount Park. Philadelphia

"From Eva"

Mailed on July 25, 1907, to Emma, who was living with the Milton C. Pyle family in West Grove, Pennsylvania.
The postcard publisher is unknown.

"F.G."

Mailed in October 1907 to Emma at home. Postcard publisher: Baehre, Th. E.L. Series 1056.

At Thanksgiving, "F.W.G." wrote Emma from the small Chester County town of Atglen. The card was designed by Ellen Hattie Clapsaddle, who was the most prolific of the American signed artists during the heyday of the postcard.[17]

In early 1908, still at home, Emma received a card from her brother William.

When summer arrived, she was living in Malvern, Pennsylvania, with the John Haines family. There she received a rather unusual card from Eva Wesley of the duck farm at Lincoln University. At the end of the nineteenth century, fluid milk dairying, market gardening, and ornamental horticulture had become important sources of farm income in southeastern Pennsylvania. These three income sources continued into the twentieth century, with the addition of poultry raising.[18]

Eva's card referenced a get-together that she, her sister Helen, and Emma were planning.

Toward Christmas, "M.B.H.," who was local and knew Helen Wesley, wrote Emma from West Grove with an invitation to visit. Emma was living in Kennett Square with the Isaac E. Chandler family.

Muckross Lake, Killarney.

"Anna"

"How are you and when are you coming down? Yours"

Mailed on November 11, 1907, to Emma at home. Postcard: Raphael Tuck & Sons' "Oilette," Regd, Postcard 7260, "Killarney," Series II.

Good Wishes for Thanksgiving Day.

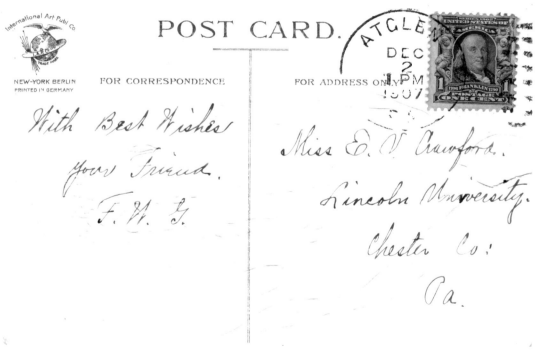

"With best wishes, your friend, F.W.G."

Mailed on December 2, 1907, to Emma at home. Postcard publisher: International Art Publ Co., New York, Berlin.

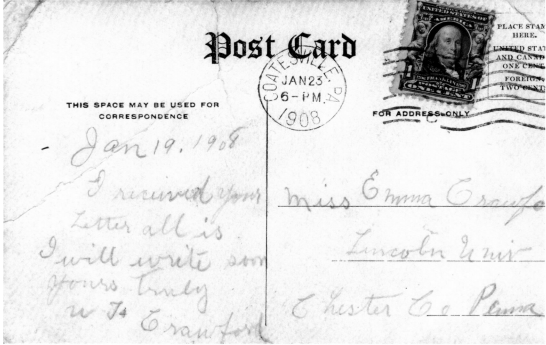

"I received your letter. All is well. I will write soon. Yours truly, W. F. Crawford"

Mailed on January 23, 1908, to Emma at home. The postcard publisher is unknown.

Raising Ducks; Lincoln University Pa.

"Dear Emma: I wrote a letter to Helen and did not write a letter to you, but I am sending this card. How are you getting along? Will be glad to see you girls, I can hardly wait until 23, be sure & come. From Eva."

Mailed during the summer of 1908 to Emma, who was living with the John Haines family in Malvern, Pennsylvania.

A year later, in 1909, three friends, "Mary, Emma, and Thelma," scrawled a cheerful Christmas greeting to Emma, who was living in Primos with the J. Wilson Howe family.

In January 1910, still living with the Howe family, Emma received a belated holiday greeting from Eva Wesley that included the not-infrequent prompt from a friend for her to write more often.

The following card, from February 1910, is one of the few in the collection that references current events. Sent from Atglen, Pennsylvania, and in handwriting that resembles F.W.G.'s, it asks "How is the strike in your city?" The general strike of 1910 was a labor strike by trolley workers of the Philadelphia Rapid Transit Company that eventually lasted until March 27 and grew to involve an estimated 140,000 people. The strike saw loss of life and property in violent standoffs between strikers, strikebreakers, and police officers, and spoke to widespread dissatisfaction with labor conditions and municipal corruption in Philadelphia.[19]

When her brother William wrote from Ercildoun in the summer of 1910, Emma was still with the J. Wilson Howe family, now living in Swarthmore.

"I may get up to Lincoln Saturday on the train. Come over some time. Had a letter from Helen. Excuse writing. Yours truly, M. B. H."

Mailed in December 1908 to Emma, who was living with the Isaac E. Chandler family in Kennett Square, Pennsylvania. Postcard publisher: PF, Series 6445.

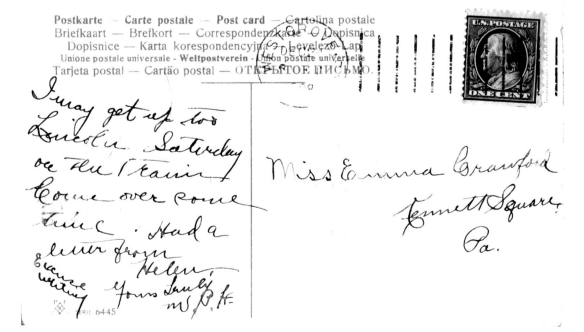

Greetings for Christmas

"Merry Xmas, Mary, Emma, Thelma"

Mailed on December 23, 1909, to Emma, who was living with the J. Wilson Howe family in Primos, Pennsylvania. The postcard publisher is unknown.

Christmas Greetings

"Hoping you a merry xmas and happy new year. Write why don't you? Burt told me he heard from you, from Eva Wesley"

Mailed in January, 1910 to Emma, who was living with the J. Wilson Howe family in Primos, Pennsylvania. The postcard publisher is unknown.

Fond Remembrance

"Friend: How is the strike in your city? Have you seen Arthur recently? Hoping you are in good spirits. Your Friend."

Mailed on February 23, 1910, to Emma, who was living with the J. Wilson Howe family in Primos, Pennsylvania. Postcard publisher: AA 631/9.

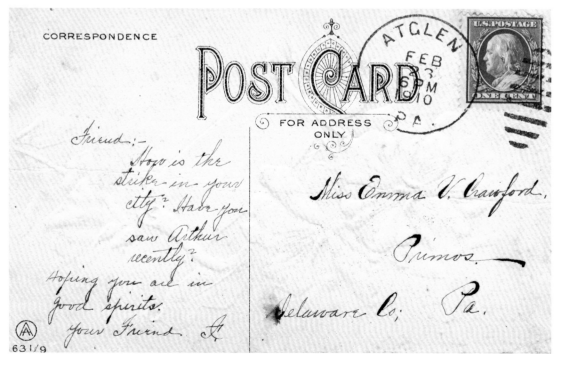

With Best Wishes!

"From your Brother W. F. Crawford. Ercildoun, Chester Co., Penna"

Mailed on June 30, 1910, to Emma, who was living with the J. Wilson Howe family in Swarthmore, Pennsylvania. Postcard publisher: P.T., Series 2995.

Postkarte — Carte postale — Post card — Cartolina postale
Briefkaart — Brefkort — Correspondenzkarte — Dopisnica
Dopisnice — Karta korespondencyjna — Levelező-Lap
Unione postale universale - **Weltpostverein** - Union postale universelle
Tarjeta postal — Cartão postal — ОТКРЫТОЕ ПИСЬМО.

Eugene Herndon Glenn, Eva Wesley's future husband, also wrote that summer, sending a picture of the beaux arts/neoclassical post office building in Atlantic City.

In the fall of 1910, when Emma was working for Woodrow Wilson, her friend Arthur wrote from Washington, DC, sending a photograph of the then-new Municipal Building, now known as the John A. Wilson District Building. Today it is part of the Pennsylvania Avenue National Historic Site.[20]

Close to Thanksgiving, Eugene Glenn wrote Emma at Prospect House in Princeton, wondering when she would be returning home. He mentioned a recent football game between Lincoln University and Philadelphia's all-Black Stentonworth Athletic Club.

An undated and apparently unmailed card from Emma to Helen Wesley suggests that late in 1910 Emma was still working for the Wilsons, while Helen had moved on to employment in Asbury Park on the New Jersey shore.

At some point after Wilson's election as governor of New Jersey in November 1910, Emma moved to another household in Princeton. The following card from Eva Wesley was addressed to her at an unspecified residence on "Morven Place," a street where several of Princeton's professors lived. Morven is a famous place name in Princeton that originally referred to a historic mansion owned by Richard Stockton III, a signer of the Declaration of Independence. By 1910 some of the land associated with the mansion had been developed into an upscale subdivision, north of the historic mansion.

It's not completely clear when Emma left the Woodrow Wilson household, but by December 31, when her friend Mary wrote her there, she had probably left New Jersey.

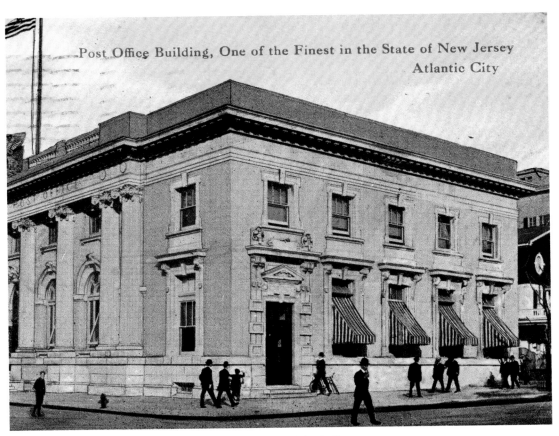

Post Office Building, One of the Finest in the State of New Jersey Atlantic City

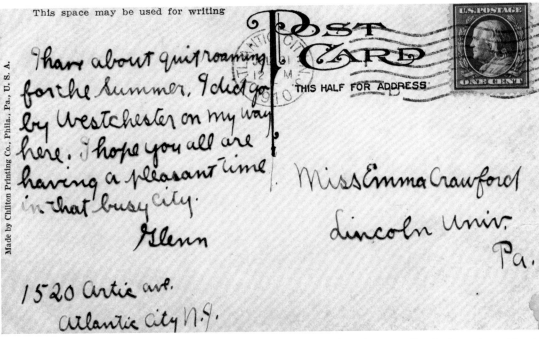

"I have about quit roaming for the summer. I did go by West Chester on my way here. I hope you all are having a pleasant time in that busy city. Glenn. 1520 Artic Ave., Atlantic City, NJ."

Mailed in July 1910 to Emma at home. Postcard publisher: Chilton Printing Co., Philadelphia

Municipal Building, Washington, D.C.

"Hello, Emma. Back here having a nice time. I suppose everything is lovely. Arthur, 417 T St., N.W."

Mailed in October 1910 to Emma, who was living with the Woodrow Wilson family in Princeton, New Jersey.
Postcard publisher: The Washington News Company, Washington, DC, No. M 1346.

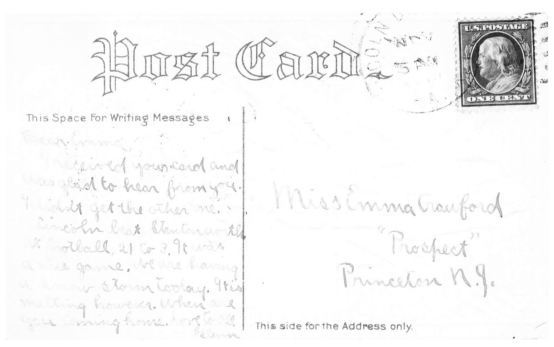

"*Dear Emma, I received your card and was glad to hear from you. I didn't get the other one. Lincoln beat Stentonworth at football, 21 to 3. It was a nice game. We are having a snow storm today. It is melting however. When are you coming home? Love to all, Glenn*"

Mailed in November 1910 to Emma, who was living with the Woodrow Wilson family in Princeton, New Jersey. The postcard publisher is unknown.

Princeton Inn, North View. Princeton, N.J.

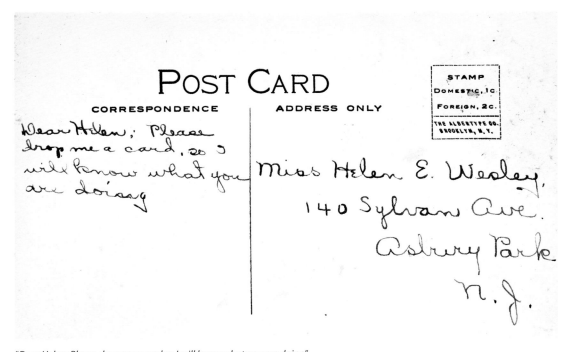

"Dear Helen: Please drop me a card so I will know what you are doing"

Postcard publisher: The Albertype Co., Brooklyn, New York.

A Kiss in Lincoln University, Penna.

"Hello Emma! How are you? I am well. How about this card: I have sent a few of different ones, sent my boy one, Arthur Frazier from Texas he is in Buffalo now. Love to see you. I wrote Helen. Moving picture in Lincoln tonight. They are in a tent. From Eva"

Mailed in 1910 to Emma, who was living in an as-yet-unidentified household in Princeton, New Jersey. The postcard publisher is unknown.

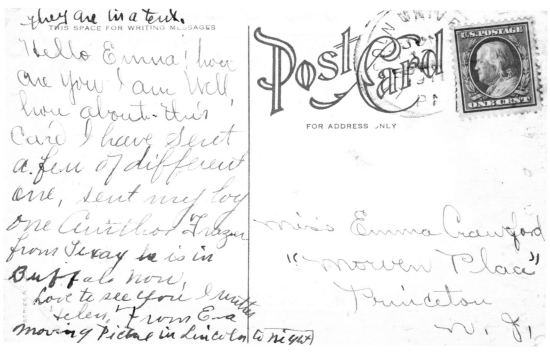

A Prosperous and Happy New Year

"Hello E. A Happy New Years. I had a bully Xmas. Several presents all just lovely. Hope you are well, I am. Best regards to all, from Mary"

Mailed on December 31, 1910, to Emma at the Woodrow Wilson household in Princeton, New Jersey (which she may have left at that point). The postcard publisher is unknown.

Chapter Five

On the Road with the Minstrel Show

The composers, the singers, the musicians, the speakers,
the stage performers—The minstrel show got them all.
—W. C. Handy, quoted in *Blacking Up: The Minstrel Show in 19th-Century America*

Emma's older brother, Merris, played in minstrel shows throughout the period of her postcard collection, and his travels throughout the country were a source of some of her most interesting postcards. Besides their visual and geographic interest, his cards give us a more nuanced understanding of what minstrelsy entailed for Black performers and their families than is generally available. This is an area about which there is limited documentation, and Merris's postcard correspondence fills in some of the gaps: documenting his travels, shedding light on the conditions of work for Black entertainers, and illustrating how family ties were maintained across wide distances.

Minstrelsy was "the first original form of American musical theater that was not imitative of traditional storytelling, formal ritual, or the European stage."[1] It has a complicated history that mirrors not only America's racism but also its fascination with Black musical and verbal forms of expression. By Merris and Emma's time, minstrel shows had dominated American musical expression for more than seventy years and were still the leading form of American popular entertainment. Minstrelsy's dominance appeared to be declining in the early 1900s, but there is evidence that it continued to remake itself throughout the first half of the twentieth century, including as part of staged school plays as well as productions and rituals in white civic and cultural life.[2]

Throughout minstrelsy's long reign, racial stereotypes that relentlessly reinforced the notion that Black people were inherently inferior to whites were an integral part of the shows. The effect on the public's concepts of Black and white identity and ideas about racial status was powerful and

Merris Porter Crawford, stage name Mike or Morris Ford, early 1900s.

Vintage Golliway soft toy. Karen Arnold, CC0, via Wikimedia Commons: https://commons. wikimedia.org/wiki/File:Vintage-golliway-soft -toy.jpg.

lasting. And it was global, because minstrel shows and minstrel imagery traveled widely outside the US. For example, French composer Claude Debussy's 1908 "Golliwogg's Cakewalk" from the Children's Corner Suite took its inspiration from the Golliwogg, a minstrel-like Black doll with red pants, red bow tie, and wild hair, and from the cakewalks that traditionally ended minstrel shows.[3]

Yet, while racially debasing, minstrel shows were also the gateway through which hundreds of Black dancers, singers, musicians, and other entertainers entered American show business for the first time on a large scale—and thereby introduced white Americans, and the world, to profoundly influential Black musical rhythms and styles.[4] For the performers, the shows represented a decent living, especially when compared to the alternatives—farming, manual labor, and domestic service.[5] They were an opportunity to travel, which for centuries had been completely denied African Americans or had been tightly controlled.[6] And they were the path to a rewarding world of comradery, creative expression, national recognition, and cheering public acclaim.

This was the irony of minstrelsy. It was a vehicle for undermining Black progress that forced Black entertainers into activities and attitudes that played into their oppression.[7] At the same time, it was a powerful outlet for Black employment and expression. Meanwhile, white and Black audiences flocked to the performances, where they absorbed a toxic blend of pernicious racial stereotypes and up-to-the-minute beats. To counter that toxicity, Black entertainers undoubtedly created their own world within minstrelsy, a world whose values respected their integrity, creativity, and racial truths, separate from whatever demeaning antics they were expected to carry out on stage. This private world of resistance and cultural meaning was essential for survival as a "nation within a nation."

Paul Laurence Dunbar's 1896 poem "We Wear the Mask" captures this duality. While Dunbar spoke of Black lives generally, he used imagery from the stage, and his words apply equally to that setting:

> We wear the mask that grins and lies,
> It hides our cheeks and shades our eyes,—
> This debt we pay to human guile;
> With torn and bleeding hearts we smile,
> And mouth with myriad subtleties.[8]

W. E. B. Du Bois's draft eulogy for the pioneering comedian and vaudevillian Bert Williams reflects a similar awareness of the complexities underlying performances that on the surface were simply amusing entertainment:

> When in the calm afterday of thought and struggle to racial peace we look back to pay tribute to those who helped most, we shall single out for highest praise those who made the world laugh, Bob Cole, Ernest Hogan, George Walker and, above all, Bert Williams. For this was not mere laughing: it was the smile that hovered above blood and tragedy, the light mask of happiness that hid breaking hearts and bitter souls.[9]

Minstrelsy's Early Years

Jim Crow, a Comic Song
Sung by Mr. Rice at the Chestnut Street Theatre

At . . . tenshun all de Univarse,
My kingdom's rite weel,
Tan by to jump "Jim Crow"
Pon de toe and heel.

Weel about and turn about and do jis so,
Eb'ry time I weel about I jump Jim Crow.

I was born in ole Werginy
A long time ago,
Wen unkel Sam made de Inemy
Jump Jim Crow.
        Weel about etc.[10]

The beginning of minstrelsy is generally traced to February 1843, when four white men, wearing ill-fitting, ragtag clothing, their faces blackened by burnt cork, took the stage in New York City to perform an evening of the "oddities, peculiarities, eccentricities, and comicalities of that Sable Genus of Humanity" ("sable" being a reference to dark-brown skin). They were an instant sensation. Very quickly, minstrelsy swept the nation and became America's favorite form of stage entertainment.[11]

White Americans' prior exposure to the style and content of Black music set the stage for the new art form's meteoric acceptance. As early as the colonial period, "black musicians provided much of the dance music for the colonists of all classes; they played for country dances, balls in the towns, and frequently for dancing schools, too." Impersonations of Black people, and particularly of Black dancing, also dated back to the 1700s.[12]

Additional groundwork for minstrelsy's acceptance was laid by T. D. Rice's impersonation of "Jim Crow" in the late 1820s, which supposedly copied the exact posture, movements, and song of an old Black man Rice had seen on the street, and unquestionably by Master Juba (William Henry Lane), a free Black man who performed in the 1840s and was thought to be "beyond question the very greatest of all dancers."[13]

As the principal Black professional minstrel before the Civil War, Master Juba served as a link between the white world and authentic Black source material.[14] He is said to be the unnamed dancer whom Charles Dickens described in *American Notes for General Circulation* as:

a lively young negro, who is the wit of the assembly, and the greatest dancer known. . . .

Single shuffle, double shuffle, cut and cross-cut; snapping his fingers, rolling his eyes, turning in his knees, presenting the backs of his legs in front, spinning about on his toes and heels like nothing but the man's fingers on the tambourine; dancing with two left legs, two right legs, two wooden legs, two wire legs, two spring legs—all sorts of legs and no legs—what is this to him?[15]

Building on the precedent-setting popularity of Jim Crow, Master Juba, and perhaps others, minstrelsy relied from the beginning on Black culture—as interpreted by whites—for its inspiration. Early white minstrels made use of Black dances and dance steps, reproduced individual Black songs and "routines" intact, absorbed African American syncopated rhythms into their music, and employed characteristically Black folk elements and forms.[16] It was an early indication of the powerful influence Black culture would have on American performing arts.

The content quickly warped into caricatures and stereotypes. From the outset minstrelsy unequivocally branded Black Americans as peculiar, comical, and inferior, thereby assuring white audiences of their racial superiority. Even sympathetic Black characters were cast as inferiors. In this respect minstrelsy was one of the first examples of the way American popular culture would exploit and manipulate Black people and their culture to please, benefit, and play up to white audiences.

In the early years of minstrelsy, characterizations of Black people were somewhat nuanced and had not settled into the later stereotypes. Early shows included such diversity as African American hunters and fishermen, flirtatious young lovers, Black frontiersmen, husbands and wives living happily together, and heartbroken lovers pining for their sweethearts. Importantly, before the mid-1850s many minstrel troupes also expressed fundamental ambivalence about slavery by portraying both positive images of happy plantation Black people and negative condemnations of the cruelty and inhumanity of slavery in the same shows.[17] With time, however, the format of shows became more formulaic and increasingly reliant on racial stereotypes like Mammy (an obese, coarse, maternal figure who had great love for her white "family" but often treated her own family with disdain), Uncle Tom (a faithful, happily submissive servant), Zip Coon (a lazy, easily frightened, chronically idle, inarticulate buffoon), the pickaninny (a coon child with bulging eyes, unkempt hair, red lips, and a wide mouth into which was stuffed huge slices of watermelon), and the brute (an innately savage, animalistic, destructive, and criminal Black man who deserved punishment, maybe even death).[18]

Stephen Foster's 1848 song "Old Uncle Ned," which mourns the death of a faithful, devoted, "happy" slave, illustrates the formula in action.[19]

Dere was an old Nigga, dey call'd him Uncle Ned.
He's dead long ago, long ago!
He had no wool on de top ob his head
De place whar de wool ought to grow.

Chorus:
Den lay down de shubble and de hoe
Hang up de fiddle and de bow:
No more work for poor Old Ned
He's gone where the good Niggas go.

When Old Ned die Massa take it mighty bad,
De tears run down like de rain;
Old missus turn pale, and she gets berry sad
Cayse she nebber see Old Ned again.

Chorus

His fingers were long like de cane in de brake,
He had no eyes for to see;
He had no teeth for eat de corn cake
So had to let de corn cake be.

Chorus

There were Black minstrel troupes as early as the 1850s, but it was not until after the Civil War that Black entertainers took to the stage in large numbers.[20] Despite the limitations of the racial stereotypes that shaped the programs, minstrelsy was a platform on which Black entertainers could demonstrate their diverse artistic talents. It was also their sole opportunity to make a regular living as entertainers, musicians, actors, or composers. Minstrelsy became a way of life for hundreds of Black entertainers in the post–Civil War period.[21] The first Black companies did not use blackface makeup, and white audiences were astonished to see that the natural skin color of African Americans ranged from deepest brown to nearly white.[22]

By the end of the 1870s, minstrel shows were among the most popular forms of entertainment, traveling on the rapidly expanding railroad system to every corner of the county. Around the same time, whites took

"Yours truly Mike"

Richards & Pringle's in Denver, Colorado, 1905.

over the most successful Black troupes. These white-owned shows, like Callender's Original Georgia Minstrels and Richards & Pringle's Georgia Minstrels, had the greatest exposure and made the most money, proving the marketability of Black entertainment for white audiences.[23]

As the number of skilled musicians grew, minstrel bands also grew and began to include a wide variety of instruments. The street parade led by the band soon became a prominent and popular feature of the show. This 1905 photographic postcard shows Richards & Pringle's Georgia Minstrels arriving in Denver, Colorado, Merris Crawford among them (probably in the second wagon). Their destination, the Tabor Grand theater, had opened in 1879 as a lavishly appointed opera house but by 1905 had transitioned to more popular forms of entertainment.[24]

Minstrelsy at the Turn of the Century

By the early 1900s, minstrel shows followed a well-established format that consisted of a series of activities—jokes, riddles, and songs—rather than a sustained story like the acts or scenes of a play.[25] Each show was organized into three sections: first, the traditional minstrel semicircle—Tambo and Bones, Mister Interlocutor, and other customary characters—who sang and told jokes to the accompaniment of a small orchestra; second, the olio, consisting of quick-paced variety acts by a wide range of entertainers, including singers, dancers, vocal quartets, acrobats, slack-wire artists, male and female impersonators, contortionists, ventriloquists, and magicians; and finally, a musical production, or afterpiece, often with a plantation setting. The roles of the singers were fixed by tradition. For example, tenors sang tear-jerking ballads, comedians were given comic songs, and specialty numbers were the domain of singers with rich, deep voices.[26] The format accommodated an enormous range of talent and covered the range from high-toned to bizarre.[27] The entertainment was fast paced, varied, and designed to appeal to a wide audience.[28]

Minstrel songs generally fell into three categories: ballads, comic songs, and specialties. Spirituals, and other religious songs, as well as operatic airs were also used. At the turn of the century, "coon songs," identifiable by their prominent, and purportedly humorous, use of the derogatory word "coon," were especially popular.[29] Typical were "Little Alabama Coon," "All Coons Look Alike to Me," and "Coon! Coon! Coon!"[30] "Coon songs and other minstrel tunes served as the centerpiece—the *pièce de resistance*—at even the most prestigious affairs, entertaining lofty white audiences," historian Lynn Hudson observes.[31]

The cakewalk was popular, as was the comic Jonah Man, who was plagued by bad luck (e.g., "They nam'd me after Papa and the same day Papa died").[32] There were also new musical forms that marked the advent of ragtime.[33] At this late stage, burnt cork makeup was used less and less by Black entertainers and was more a matter of individual preference than a requirement. In fact, there were probably more whites doing blackface acts than Black people. Black performers who *did* appear in blackface were usually comedians, who used burnt cork to enhance the visual contrast between their comedic character, typically clothed in baggy clothes and floppy shoes, and his dapper, well-dressed partner, or "straight man," who was frequently of a very light complexion.[34]

By the turn of the century, professional Black companies had refined the street parade and its component performances into a fine art designed to bait the public's interest in the evening's minstrel show. The parades were all-day affairs that featured brass bands, men in top hats, eccentric "walking gents," exotic animals, a joy wagon with "funny boys," and a "rube" or "pickaninny" band.[35]

W. C. Handy, who got his start in minstrelsy and later distinguished himself as the "Father of the Blues," described one such procession:

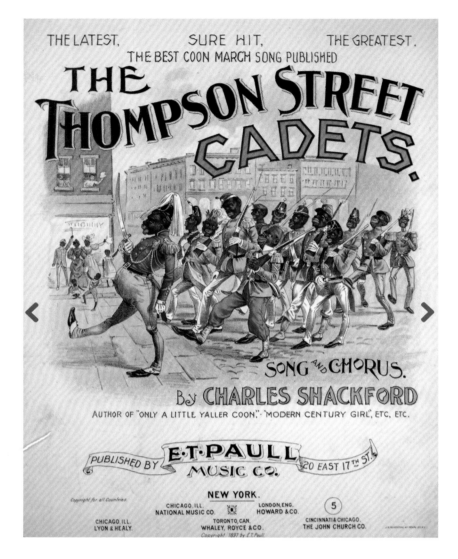

"The Best Coon March Song Published": The Thompson Street Cadets, by Charles Shackford, 1897. Johns Hopkins University. (n.d.). *The Thompson Street Cadets. The Latest, The Greatest, Sure Hit, The Best Coon March Song Published.* Retrieved August 10, 2020, from https://images.app.goo.gl/RhVRomB6cTkXKabc7.

The parade itself was headed by the managers in their four-horse carriages. Doffing silk hats and smiling their jeweled smiles, they acknowledged with easy dignity the small flutter of polite applause their high-stepping horses provoked. After them came the carriage in which the stars rode. The "walking gents" followed, that exciting company which included comedians, singers, and acrobats. They in turn were followed by the drum major—not an ordinary drum major beating time for a band, mind you, but a performer out of the books, an artist with the baton. His twirling stick suggested a bicycle wheel revolving in the sun. Occasionally he would give it a toss and then recover the glistening affair with the same flawless skill. The drum major in a minstrel show was a character to conjure with; not infrequently he stole the parade. Our company had two such virtuosi; in addition to twirling their batons, they added the new wrinkle of tossing them back and forth to each other as they marched.[36]

The parade might be followed by a challenge baseball game, with members of the troupe squaring off against a local team (which even in southern states might be white or include white players). In the evening there would be an outdoor orchestral concert, followed by the actual show.[37] It's not hard to imagine the curiosity and excitement these festivities stimulated, certainly in any small town, but especially where Black faces were a novelty.

Although Black minstrels' pay was modest, and less than what comparable white performers received, the salary always included room, board, and travel. For instance, when W. C. Handy started out as a musician with Mahara's Minstrels in 1896, his weekly pay was $6, which was less than the average nonagricultural wage for this period of about $9.40 weekly, but which included "cakes" (i.e., food), plus room and board.[38] The total package provided more security than he would have had in most other jobs.

Ultimately, minstrelsy was the incubator for many artistic forms of the twentieth century. In addition to W. C. Handy, alumni included Gussie L. Davis, the first Black man to succeed in Tin Pan Alley; Bert Williams, a star of musicals, vaudeville, and the Ziegfeld Follies; Gertrude "Ma" Rainey and Bessie Smith, the Queens of the Blues; and Jelly Roll Morton, one of the founders of modern jazz.[39] Theater critic Edith Isaacs noted that this was "[a time] when the Negro was gradually to slough off the caricature of himself in blackface and to try his hand at serious playwriting and composition. There were many gifted men among the comedians, the dancers, [and] composers."[40]

Meanwhile, within Black communities there was a wide range of musical activity during this vital period, including vocal quartets, string bands, mandolin clubs, and brass bands. These groups performed for all kinds of occasions, from funerals to serenading parties and "rag" dances. Black community music was highly eclectic and, like minstrelsy, contained the seeds of almost every American music style that would subsequently emerge in the twentieth century.[41]

"Mike Ford," Black Musician

Under the professional name of Mike or Morris Ford (Ford being his mother's maiden name), Emma's older brother, Merris, played tuba and baritone horn during the 1900s and 1910s with several minstrel companies.

"Snake charmer: Ringlers [sic]*, Barnum & Bailey" "Property of Merris Ford Sideshow Band"* (on the reverse).

An unmailed card from Merris to his mother (probably included in a letter). Postcard publisher: The Ridenour Photographic Studio, Philadelphia.

His work took him to Europe and Canada, and throughout the United States, far from his roots in the tiny Chester County village of Kelton. Before going on the road, he had most likely started his musical career with one of the many "colored bands" that provided entertainment at local events in Pennsylvania's Black and white communities.

In these later decades of minstrelsy's popularity, many of the jobs were in small southern, midwestern, and western towns, as Merris's postcards document. Reaching these communities, and traveling on the road in general, was not easy. The schedule was typically an endless series of one-nighters, accommodations were often poor-quality wooden housing that was subject to fires, and there was a chance of managers and agents skipping out with the money. In every town the entertainers had to find restaurants that would serve them, which was often quite difficult.[42] On top of all of this, they faced both the physical dangers of hazardous nineteenth- and early twentieth-century rail and road travel and the additional possibility of humiliating or even life-threating encounters with white travelers and town residents.[43]

These risks were fully illustrated in a 1909 report to the *Indianapolis Freeman*, which followed the national music scene closely. A correspondent wrote, "[The Smart Set] company has been playing one-night stands . . . in the heart of the South. . . . In some towns they were unable to obtain anything to eat or a place to lodge; then making 4 o'clock trains in the morning and these trains averaging ten miles an hour, taking all day to cover forty miles, often too late for a matinee. At one place the men had to make a guard line around the women to keep the white men from assaulting them, and they all carry .48 revolvers." The story concluded with what was probably the most feasible solution within the constraints of Jim Crow: "In going over this route everyone was satisfied that a blunder had been made in sending them without a private [railroad] car."[44]

The first public record of Merris Crawford's career appeared in the May 6, 1905, edition of the *Indianapolis Freeman*. Merris was playing at the time with Al E. Holman's Band and Serenaders, who were employed by the J. T. McCaddon Company, also known as the McCaddon Circus and International Show. His experience with the J. T. McCaddon Company illustrates both the glamour of being a bandsman—the tour took him to Europe—and the uncertainty of the work.

> Notes from Al. E. Holman's Band and Serenaders, now touring Europe with the J. T. McCaddon's Company. Walter Brister, our band leader has made quite a hit with the French musicians on account of the manner in which his band handles ragtime. It is something new and the entire colored Company, Billy Banks, T. Peterson, James Chapman, L. H. Randolph, John E. Ritter, John Tobias, George Sebastian, Morris Ford . . . is a treat to the French.[45]

The McCaddon Company was supposed to tour Europe for five years, but instead it folded after just a few months. On October 1, 1905, the *New York Times* reported that it had collapsed in Grenoble, France, "after a season of continuous misfortune." Two hundred fifty men, women, and children were stranded—with Merris presumably among them. When McCaddon attempted to return to New York on the liner *St. Louis*, he was arrested on a charge of fraudulent bankruptcy. Meanwhile, it was only thanks to contributions from the sympathetic American public that the circus members were able to book return passage to the US. [46] Related by marriage to James A. Bailey, McCaddon was also the business manager of P. T. Barnum and James A. Bailey's circus before its merger with Ringling Brothers in 1907.[47] His business skills apparently served him better in that role.

After the McCaddon debacle, and for several years following, Merris played regularly with Richards & Pringle's Georgia Minstrels (routinely misspelled as Richard & Pringle's). It was a wildly popular all-Black company, founded in 1883 by two white men, Orrin E. Richards and Charles W. Pringle, that routinely played to packed houses. In contrast to McCaddon's Company, Richards & Pringle's Georgia Minstrels offered Merris steady employment with a successful professional organization. The company's popularity ensured adoring audiences, sold-out houses, the opportunity to play with some of the country's best musicians, singers, and stage performers, and travel on dedicated Pullman railway cars. "Community musical organizations treated members of Richards and Pringle's Georgia Minstrels like visiting royalty."[48]

Despite the racist material, Black minstrel shows like Richards & Pringle's invariably drew large audiences from the Black community (note the segregated seating referenced in the newspaper advertisement). What was the attraction? Because racial stereotypes were such a pervasive element of everyday life, it is likely that Black audiences acknowledged the necessity of overlooking them in order to enjoy the songs, dances, acrobatics, and overall entertainment. Some would revel in, and be inspired by, the amazing artistry of the performers. Some would understand the ways—both witting and unwitting—that the performers themselves used various aspects of their artistry to subvert or critique minstrelsy's racism. Sadly, some, in a manifestation of internalized racism—ideas, beliefs, actions and behaviors that support or collude with racism—might even have accepted the stereotypes as true in part or in whole.

In any event, the shows were a chance for Black Americans to see their own people onstage, comically or dramatically costumed, with or without blackface makeup, and performing catchy songs and dances with great skill. It was entertainment for the common man, who was not concerned that, as W. C. Handy observed, a "large section of upper-crust Negroes" strongly condemned the material.[49] Black minstrels were so popular with Black audiences that in order to fill more seats some theater owners even took the radical step of letting Black patrons sit outside "N----r Heaven" in the upstairs gallery. Of the all-Black shows, Richards & Pringle's had the largest and most loyal Black following. For example, playing in Memphis in the fall of 1896, "Richards & Pringle's Georgia Minstrels succeeded in drawing . . . in the neighborhood of 5,000 people—4,000 Negroes and 1,000 Whites, the largest indoor paid audience ever known in that city," the *Indianapolis Freeman* reported.[50]

The band was a central component of a Richards & Pringle's show. The musicians were versatile and hardworking and usually expected to play more than one instrument. The performances also showcased a wealth of other Black entertainers, including singers, dancers, jugglers, and acrobats. Adding to the popularity of the shows was the charisma of their star comedian, Billy Kersands. Storied as a "nature-gifted" performer, in 1880 Kersands introduced "Mary's Gone wid a Coon," a forerunner of the "coon song" phenomenon described earlier.[51] One of his specialties was the "Essence of Virginny," a folksy dance that required a nimble "combination of knee work and head buttoning to keep time with the music." The other star of the show was Clarence Powell, singer and comedian, whose "old mammy" character left people "in convulsions every night."[52]

Many have observed the power of Black laughter as a tool for psychological survival and to confront oppression and hardship.[53] In the context of minstrelsy, humor served multiple purposes. In addition to lifting the spirits of audiences, it was an acceptable avenue for poking fun at both white and Black behavior, making sly social observations, and commenting on life's contradictions and absurdities. In a world with no radio broadcasts and little competition from vinyl recordings or movies (both still in their infancy), the men and women who could make people laugh were among the highest-paid members of minstrel troupes. For example, a 1915 obituary for Richards & Pringle's Billy Kersands—"one of the foremost negro minstrels of the world"—reported that "he drew large salaries and larger percentages" and "had his own private car on the Railroad occupied by his family and no one else."[54]

◆ ◆ ◆

Merris wrote his mother and sister frequently from the road, often sending colorful illustrations of the local scenery. He and his wife, Edna, traveled together, which suggests that she was a performer too. Spouses who weren't entertainers waited at home, as can be gleaned from contemporary articles and statements, such as "once a month you see your wife," in the poetic recitation called "A Showman's Dream."[55] To answer Merris's letters and cards, his mother could use the *Indianapolis Freeman*'s office, which served as a central mailbox for traveling musicians. Alternatively, he sometimes provided a forwarding address.

One of the first cards in Emma's collection was the one earlier in this chapter that Merris sent home in 1905, showing the arrival of Richards & Pringle's band in Denver. The back is addressed to their mother, Isabella Crawford, with the description "Colored" beneath her name. It is the only card in the collection with a racial designation of this type. The purpose could not have been to distinguish their mother from another Isabella Crawford living in Lincoln University, as she was the only one. Rather, the description is a casual, yet vivid, reminder of their deeply divided, racially segregated world.

Another early card is the one Merris sent their mother in February 1906, when he was on tour in the western states. The West was still the American frontier—for example, Flagstaff's population was less than two thousand people.

The minstrels' performance was praised in the local paper, the *Coconino Sun*, which noted that it was "a performance free from all objectionable features." I suspect this referred to an absence of bawdy humor or rude noises like belching and passing gas; racist humor would no doubt have been acceptable—and expected.[56]

> Something to amuse the ladies and children is always interesting. The Richards & Pringle's Famous Georgia Minstrels, who come to the opera house on Saturday, February 17, have arranged a program in the neatest and most attractive manner to suit the ladies and the little ones. The matinees given by this organization are a special feature and are largely patronized, as the reputation of this company for giving a performance free from all objectionable

"*Mrs. Isabella Crawford, Colored, Lincoln University, Chester Co. Penna.*"

They call me "Satan"

"*Dear Mother—all is well. I am still looking for a letter from you. Yours truly Mike.*"

An unmailed card dated February 19, 1906, and addressed to Isabella Crawford. (It was probably included in a letter). The publisher is unknown.

features has long been established. There will be plenty of beautiful scenery, handsome costumes and lots of music and a big lot of fun.[57]

The following postcard that Merris sent his mother in August 1906, from Fernie, British Columbia, is notable for several reasons. Published in England, it depicts a white couple in what seems to be a satirical reinterpretation of a love song, with the woman waiting for her man "in de old place, all alone," about to clobber him across the head with a broom. The card was produced by the Bamforth Company, which was known for its humorous cards on domestic and social subjects, and it was in keeping with a tradition of saucy postcards that was central to twentieth-century British popular culture.[58] The postcard is a photograph, not a drawing, either taken at, or representing, a live show. Viewing it, Merris's mother could feel she was seeing the performance in person.

Probing more deeply, it turns out that "I'se A'Waitin' for Yer Josie" was actually a "coon" song. Thus, the card was an indication of how fully American minstrelsy had been integrated into British popular culture.[59] The full lyrics reveal its roots.

I'se A'Waitin' for Yer Josie

Twas a June afternoon, and a sentimental coon
Stood alone in the shadow of the trees
There was no-one around, and you couldn't hear a sound
'Cept the hummin' and the buzzin' of the bees
You can guess I suppose, at the reason why he chose
To be there, if you can't, then I'll explain
He had to come to meet a gal, but she wasn't punctual
So the coon began to murmur in a melancholy strain,

"I'se a-waiting for yer Josie
In the old place all alone
And I want yer, want yer, want yer just to tell me
That you love me and you're my own
I'm so lonely, lonely, lonely, Josie Dear, waitin' all alone for you
Drop your occupation, and take a short vacation
And bring me consolation Josie, do."[60]

Also noteworthy is that the woman standing on the chair is a crudely disguised man. Male and female impersonators, playing for laughs, were common in British music halls, as they were in minstrelsy.[61] In American minstrelsy, female impersonation by male actors had a long history, dating

I'se A'Waitin' For Yer Josie. I'se a'waitin' –
waitin' – /Waitin' – for yer Josie, In de old
place, all alone.

I'SE A'WAITIN' FOR YER JOSIE.
I'se a'waitin' – waitin' –
Waitin' – for yer Josie,
In de old place, all alone.

*"All is well. Regards to friends. Yours as ever.
M. P. Ford"*

Mailed August 6, 1906, to Isabella Crawford
at home. Postcard publisher: Bamforth,
Photo., Holmfirth, Yorkshire.

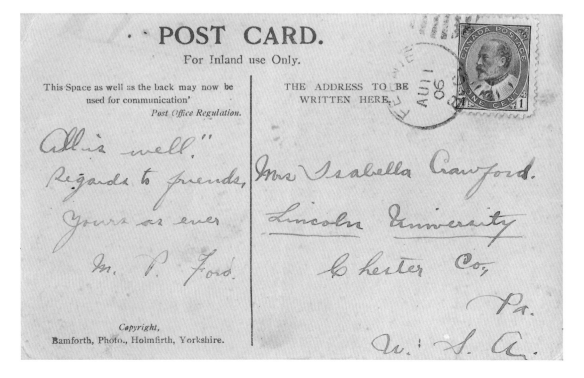

BLUE BELL.

Blue Bell

"Sweet Bill"

An unmailed card. Postcard publisher:
Bamforth, New York City. "Life Model Series."

to George Christy's depiction of Miss Lucy Long, a flirtatious mixed-race woman, in the 1840s. Typical impersonated female roles were dark-skinned "Mammy," who was maternal, comical, and sexually unattractive, and her counterpart, lighter-skinned "Jezebel," who was mixed-race, beautiful, and sexually available. These and other slavery era stereotypes of Black women were reinforced by minstrelsy and popular entertainment long after Emancipation and, in fact, continue to populate media depictions of Black women.[62] This includes the comedic portrayal of Mammy-like figures by many of today's Black male actors.[63]

Merris's card of "Blue Bell" is another example of cross-dressing humor, courtesy again of Bamforth. In postcards' golden era, many of the top impersonators—both male and female—appeared on souvenir cards that featured the leading lights of British and American theater.[64]

Will No One Play With Me?

"Portland Oregon September 26/06. I just received the letter you wrote to Revelstoke, B.C. Regards to friends. Mike"

Mailed on September 26, 1906, to Emma at home. Postcard: The Rotograph Co., New York City.

In September 1906, Merris wrote his sister from Portland, Oregon. In later years Portland would be dubbed "the whitest city in America," because of its history of entrenched racism.[65] When Merris visited in 1906, it was entering a period of rapid growth and housed large numbers of sailors and gold rush miners who would surely have welcomed the entertainment provided by Richards & Pringle's. Interestingly, when Merris retired from music, he settled in Portland, despite the city's reputation.

Richards & Pringle's 1906 western tour got its usual good press reviews, such as this article from Salem, Oregon's *Daily Capital Journal*:

Two and a half hours of fun is promised on Friday night at the Grand opera house when Richards & Pringle's famous Georgia minstrels will hold the boards. This is the only minstrel company extant composed exclusively of

Shasta Springs, Calif.

"Dunsmuir California Oct. Yours truly Mike."

Mailed on October 19, 1906, to Emma at home. The postcard publisher is unknown.

genuine negroes. The performance is a novelty and differs almost entirely from those given by burnt cork Caucasians in the same role. The fun and music by the dusky Africans is of the spontaneous kind and it is claimed the performance is "Better than a circus."[66]

In October 1906, Merris was in California, where he played at Shasta Springs, a popular summer resort during the late nineteenth and early twentieth centuries, on the Upper Sacramento River. The resort was on the main line of the Southern Pacific Railroad, and natural springs on the property were the original sources of the water and beverages that became known as the Shasta brand of soft drinks.[67]

In December 1906, still in northern California, Merris sent Emma a card from Cloverdale, a small town on the Russian River, and one of the stops on the San Francisco and Northern Pacific Railway.

The year 1907 took Merris to the South first, followed by a swing through the Midwest and a return to the West. In February, Richards & Pringle's gave an afternoon concert in Fort Worth, Texas, that reflects the range of material, from classical to popular, that made up minstrel bands' repertoires.

A Merry Xmas From . . .

"Cloverdale Cal—Dec 20th/06. Yours truly Mike. Hello Mother, look for a letter."

Mailed December 20, 1906, to Emma at home. The postcard publisher is unknown.

Program
"Lights Out"   March
Selection   Johnny Jones
"Fall of Jericho" Descriptive   Polly Phonia
    Overture Sextette
Intermezzo   Cavalier Rusticana [*sic*]
Indian Dance
"Star Spangled Banner"[68]

In April, now in Charleston, South Carolina, Merris sent a birds-eye view of the city to his mother, who—along with his sister—was living with the Milton Pyle family in West Grove. Of Richards & Pringle's South Carolina tour, the *New York Dramatic Mirror* reported that they played a good house in Charleston with a "satisfactory performance" and did fair business and "pleased" in Columbia.[69]

June 1907 found Merris in Michigan and Minnesota. By this time Emma had left the Pyle household and was now employed by the John Remsen family in West Grove, Pennsylvania. A card Merris sent Emma on June 1 depicts the breakwater of Marquette, Michigan, a town in Michigan's Upper

Birds Eye View, Charleston, S.C.

"April 14/07. With best wishes from yours truly Mike."

Mailed on April 15, 1907, to Isabella Crawford, who was living with the Pyle family in West Grove, Pennsylvania.
Postcard publisher: Souvenir Post Card Co., New York and Berlin, No. 1604

New Breakwater and Lights, Marquette, Mich.

"Will write soon. Your letter rec—Yours truly M.P.F."

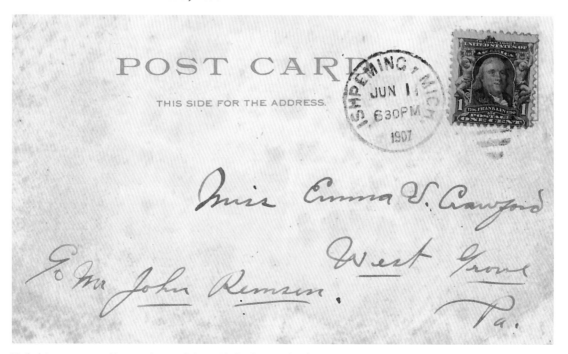

Mailed June 1, 1907, to Emma, who was living with the Remsen family in West Grove, Pennsylvania. Postcard publisher: Detroit Publishing Co., #10017

Peninsula that was a popular summer resort at the turn of the century as well as a center for iron production and distribution.

His next card was from the town of Superior, in northwestern Wisconsin, which shares Lake Superior with Marquette. Thomson Dam, pictured on the card, was constructed in 1907 by the Great Northern Power Company and was a monumental achievement for the era.[70] It is still in operation.

In the summer of 1907, Richards & Pringle's played venues throughout the state of Montana. From Harlem, Merris sent Emma a postcard photographed by Sumner Matteson, the producer of some of the earliest photographic essays on the changing American West. For Emma, the fearsome buffalo depicted on the card would have been dramatic proof that Montana was still the wild frontier. In fact, it had been a state for less than twenty years. Harlem was a tiny town near the Canadian border that had fewer than five hundred residents at the time—showing once again how the tendrils of minstrelsy reached even the most obscure byways of North America.

By August, Merris was in Olympia, Washington. His card of the Tumwater Falls, a series of cascades on the Deschutes River, shows the dam and hydroelectric power plant constructed there by the Olympia Light and Power Company, proud technological developments of the late nineteenth century.[71] The image captures a change that was taking place throughout the country as the harnessing of natural forces to serve twentieth-century industry would forever transform once-quiet wildernesses where wildlife had roamed freely.

August also took Merris to British Columbia. The buildings depicted on his card were constructed in 1905 to house the Canadian National Exhibition. New Westminster's trolley system, in the foreground, dated back to 1891.[72]

In September, Merris returned to California. The cards he sent Emma included a pleasant street scene of Vacaville, at one time the state's fresh-fruit capital, and a dramatic panoramic photograph of the San Francisco fire.

The San Francisco card was from Charles Weidner's large collection of photographic images of the April 18, 1906, earthquake, one of the most significant disasters of all time. The frequently quoted number of seven hundred deaths caused by the earthquake and fire is now believed to underestimate the total loss of life by a factor of three or four. Firestorms fed by fierce winds raged in the city for three days, causing most of the damage, and blackening an area of 4.7 square miles, or 508 city blocks.[73]

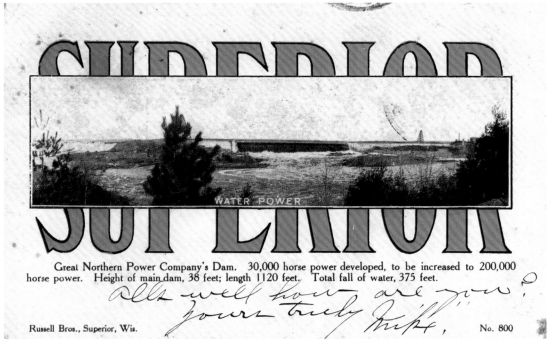

Superior Water Power. Great Northern Power Company's Dam. 30,000 horse power developed, to be increased to 200,000 horse power. Height of main dam, 38 feet; length 1120 feet. Total fall of water, 375 feet. "Alls well how are you? Yours truly Mike."

Mailed on June 16, 1907, to Emma, who was living with the Remsen family in West Grove, Pennsylvania. Postcard publisher: Russell Bros., Superior, Wisconsin, No. 800.

King of American Beasts

"Yours Mike Harlem, Mont—."

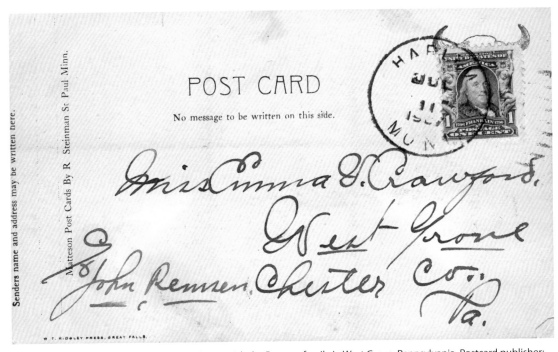

Mailed on July 11, 1907, to Emma, who was living with the Remsen family in West Grove, Pennsylvania. Postcard publisher: Matteson Post Cards by R. Steinman, St. Paul, Minnesota.

513 — UPPER TUM WATER FALLS, OLYMPIA, WASHINGTON.

Upper Tum Water Falls, Olympia, Washington

"Aug 25 – 07. Yours truly, M.P. Ford"

Mailed on August 26, 1907, to Emma at home. Postcard publisher: Edward H. Mitchell, San Francisco, no. 513.

Exhibition Buildings in Queen's Park, New Westminster, B.C.

Text illegible.

Mailed in August 1907 to Emma at home. Postcard publisher: J. J. Mackay & Co., New Westminster, British Columbia.

Exhibition Buildings in Queen's Park, New Westminster, B.C.

"Residence Street, Vacaville, Cal."

"Sept – 25 – 07. Regards to friends. Yours truly Mike."

Mailed on September 26, 1907, to Emma at home. Postcard publisher: Published for E. Edstrom by Rosin & Co., Philadelphia & New York, No. 812.

Panorama of San Francisco, California, April 18, 1906. Showing the fire.

"Oct 4/07 Dear Sister all is well. How are you? Regards to friends. Yours truly Mike" (front)

"We play at the Los Angeles Theatre in Los Angeles Calif. the week of October 20" (back)

Mailed on October 4, 1907, to Emma at home. Postcard publisher: Chas. Weidner, San Francisco, California, No. 209.

October 19, 1907

The Dramatic Review (San Francisco, California): Richards & Pringle's Georgia Minstrels.

The first minstrel show of the season had a very auspicious opening in the city last Sunday night. . . . It has been a good many years since San Francisco has seen a colored minstrel, or a white minstrel company for that matter, of the merit that characterizes Richards & Pringle's Georgia Minstrels.

San Francisco gets all sorts of minstrels in the course of the season, but there has not been a single company, in our way of thinking, that has given a better show in all respects than this same colored aggregation. We sat it through from beginning to end and enjoyed every minute of it. The big feature of the show is Clarence Powell, who is a monologue artist of no mean merit. He has an easy flowing style and a fund of infectious humor. One or two of the end men are evidently of the Billy Kersands school, for their facial grimaces are certainly startlingly effective. The variety section is particularly good. . . . The performance concludes with a musical afterpiece entitled Jim Jackson's Trip Abroad. This is a riot of blackface fun and frolic, singing and dancing, and concludes the performance which will prove to be the best the West will see this season.[74]

November took Merris to Southern California, where he sent Emma cards of Santa Monica and Los Angeles. In the early twentieth century, Santa Monica was a small resort town, growing in popularity because of its agreeable climate.[75] In 1907 the population was about seven thousand. Meanwhile, the area around Los Angeles was still mostly farmland, but the population was growing rapidly, thanks in part to "an extensive transcontinental network of railroad companies and eastern banking houses that had crystallized during the height of railroad expansion in the mid-nineteenth century."[76] The mixture of horses, trolley, and automobiles depicted in the card illustrates a city that was clearly in a period of social and economic transition.

Merris may have spent the winter of 1907–8 in California, because he and his wife Edna wrote Emma and her mother from San Bernardino in February. In the last decades of the nineteenth century, the Santa Fe, Union Pacific, and Southern Pacific railway companies had made San Bernardino the hub of their Southern California operations, paving the way for its evolution into an enterprising city. When the Santa Fe Railway established a transcontinental link in 1886, the already-prosperous valley exploded. Even more settlers flocked from the East, and population figures doubled between 1900 and 1910.[77]

Southern Pacific Train and Grounds at Santa Monica, Cal.

"Nov 26 – 11/07. Winter time in California" (front)

"Yours truly M.P. Ford. #1106 San Pedro St., Los Angeles Calif. (back)

Mailed on November 26, 1907, to Emma at home. Postcard publisher: Newman Post Card Co., Los Angeles, California, No. 5382.

Broadway North from 4th st., Los Angeles, Cal.

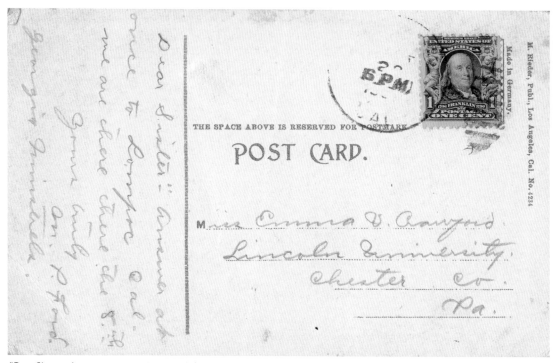

"Dear Sister—Answer at once to Lompoc Cal. We are there there [sic] the 8th. Yours truly M. P. Ford Georgia Minstrels."

Mailed in late 1907 to Emma at home. Postcard publisher: M. Rieder, Publ., Los Angeles, California, No. 4234.

450 — VIEW IN CITY PARK, SAN BERNARDINO, CALIFORNIA.

View in City Park, San Bernardino, California

"This is the City Park Building, in rear is where we are showing at." (front)

"Feb 18 /08 Yours truly, Mike (back)

Mailed on February 19, 1908, to Emma at home. Postcard publisher: E.P. Charlton & Co, Los Angeles, California, No. 450.

In February, Merris's wife, Edna, contributed a rather gruesome photographic card of a rabbit drive to Emma's collection. Rabbit drives were regularly organized by ranchers to clear their farmland of jackrabbits, which they viewed as pests. In California the drives dated to the 1870s. One observer commented, "If [the rabbits] are in good condition, some are dressed and shipped to market, where they find a ready sale. But usually the drives are carried on solely for the purpose of exterminating the pests."[78]

For a period in 1908, Merris joined the minstrel band that accompanied James M. Ferdon, a huckster notorious throughout the Midwest and West as the Great Fer-Don, "the Great Paul," or "Brother Paul."[79] Like other medicine-show operators, Ferdon relied on Black musicians, singers, comedians, and novelty acts to warm up the crowds before delivering his pitch about miraculous medical remedies and elixirs. "[Ferdon] toured the Midwest with an African American quartet dressed in the latest fashion: bulldog yellow shoes, three-inch collars, and wide-brimmed fedoras for the men, leg o'mutton sleeves, wasp waists, and peek-a-boo hats for the

Rabbit Drive in California.

"Dear Mother I will write to you soon give my love to Sister Emma. I [illegible] you Edna Crawford"

Mailed on February 25, 1908, to Isabella Crawford at home. Postcard publisher: Howard H. Mitchell, San Francisco, No. 685.

women. Ferdon was one of the few medicine showmen who had a mixed-race troupe. They were quite a spectacle in [regions] that didn't see many African Americans."[80]

To secure his audience's attention, Ferdon showered them with cash. In addition to traditional medicine-show potions, he also offered what he termed ultramodern "bloodless surgery" and claimed to work with European doctors who "could cure the most serious medical problems: Complete blindness and deafness. Paralysis. Gallstones. Appendicitis. Tumors. Cancer. All without a scalpel or the loss of a single drop of blood. . . . His audiences simply didn't see there was something discordant about world-class physicians teaming up with a man running a cornball show crafted to appeal to yokels."[81]

THE GREAT FERDON CO. NO. 2

The company is drawing large crowds nightly at Chico, Cal. Morris P. Ford and Mr. Venerable, of the Ferdon company, were the guests of Mr. Freeman, of Chico, on Sunday. Mr. Freeman is quite a talker, and loves to discuss the race question. Mrs. Breeden, a talented colored pianist, rendered some choice selections for our benefit, and we spent a very pleasant evening.[82]

For years, Ferdon operated just one step ahead of the law. The year before Merris worked for him, he had been jailed in Portland, Oregon, for practicing medicine without a license; following his release he was arrested a month later in Salt Lake City. In 1910 there was a warrant for his arrest in Sacramento for conspiracy with intent to defraud. Nonetheless, he resurfaced a few years later as "the Great La Vita," head of the Great La Vita Medicine Company, and advertised in an African American newspaper for "colored performers." All told—and fortunately—Merris worked for him for less than a year.

In July 1908 Edna and Merris were in Stockton, California, with Ferdon. Later in the year, they were with him in Berkeley, California. The card below was striking for the angelic figures that presented several views of the University of California, which was just forty years old that year. When she received it, Emma was working for the Isaac E. Chandler family in Kennett Square, Pennsylvania.

In 1909 Merris returned to Richards & Pringle's. A roster published in the *Indianapolis Freeman* illustrated the size of the show and variety of talent involved for a circuit that included stops in Arkansas, Michigan, Indiana, Oklahoma, and Texas.[83]

Greetings from Berkeley, Cal. University of California, Statue at the Entrance of University of Calif, Stiles Hall

"*Dear Sister, your letter received will answer soon. This is from Essie who sends love and will write soon. Regards to friends. Yours truly Mike & Essie [Edna Crawford] c/o Fer-don Med Co. Berkeley, Cal.*"

Mailed on December 5, 1908, to Emma, who was living with the Chandler family in Kennett Square, Pennsylvania. Postcard publisher: I. Scheff & Bros., San Francisco, Berlin, Prag.

RICHARDS & PRINGLE'S MINSTRELS

Holland & Filkings, Mgrs.

The roster is as follows:
Chas. Davis, Agent.
Band—J. A. Watts, Band Master; Fred Simpson, Geo. A. Williams, Willie Srigg, W. A. Robinson, E. B. Blake, Lloyd Cooper, Morris Ford, Walter Watkins, Frank Terry, Elmer Clay, A. Williams, Leonard Gaines, Sylvester Williams, C. R. Jones, Fred Clay, J. Johnson.
Olio, specialty acts, saxophone quartette—Fred Simpson, Walter Watkins, George Williams, Leonard Gaines.
Monologue—Clarence Powell.
White and Washington, comedians, singers, dancers.
Alabama Comedy Quartette—Kid Langford, Dave Smith, Chas. Wilson, Jokie Smith
Fred Simpson, trombone virtuoso.
Billy King and his big 3 song and dance, "Georgia Flirtation."
End Men—Clarence Powell, Billy King, Kid Langford, Dave Smith, Tom White, Billy Washington, Charlie Wilson, Alonzo Williams, Happy Beamegard, Ed Stroughter.
Singers—Sydney Kirkpatrick, Major Daniels, Jack Johnson, Jakey Smith, J. D. Proser, Monroe Saber, John Watts.
After Piece—A Military Burlesque set music, entitled "Blackville Guards."

This aggregation will appear in Indianapolis Friday evening, Aug. 6, at Tomlison Hall.
Grand street parade at noon.

An effusive review by Sylvester Russell, the *Indianapolis Freeman*'s acerbic music critic, called special attention to several features of Richards & Pringle's 1909 show, including "the largest and most tuneful male chorus thus far heard in minstrelsy," the "new and gorgeous" costumes, and "the greatest comedians, dancers, singers and yodelers that can be obtained from any part of the universe."[84] Considered to be "the dean of Black entertainment critics," Russell could be unsparing in his commentary.[85]

Advertisement. (1909, February 14). *The Daily Ardmoreite*. Retrieved May 26, 2020, from Library of Congress, Chronicling America: https://chroniclingamerica.loc.gov/lccn/sn85042303/1909-02-14/ed-1/seq-7/.

However, he praised Holland and Filkins, Richards & Pringle's managers, for their efforts to replace traditional minstrelsy with high-quality entertainment, and concluded his article triumphantly:

> No male chorus will be more tuneful. No better dancers can be possible, and no better looking, better dressed, or better behaved men can be found in the show business. . . . The general opinion is that this company will put a new spirit of popularity in the return of genuine colored minstrels as a favorite national permanent first-class theatre attraction, for it has now been discovered that the rumor of white comedians being genuine and more natural than the Negro was only a delusion.[86]

In September, Merris was in San Antonio, Texas. At the time of his visit, the Alamo mission was being managed by the Daughters of the Republic of Texas. Texas had been a state for sixty-four years.

Leading lady with Cameron Opera Company, at Robison Opera House, Saturday February 20th.

their white competitors, is strictly clean and refined. Not a suggestive word, song, joke or action can find

SELLES & BEAUX, SONG AND DANCE, WITH RICHARD & PRINGLES FAMOUS MINSTRELS, ROBISON OPERA HOUSE, TOMORROW NIGHT

to catch its breath, then feel a strong desire to rush from the auditorium in horror.

The stage of this country has seen some strange sights and theatrical folks are now waiting for this newest fantasy, this play of the terrible,

place in their program. That is probably the reason they always draw such large houses.

Ask any minstrel manager the competitor he most fears in a business fight and he will answer without hesitation, Richards & Pringle's.

In October, still in Texas, Merris sent Emma cards from Galveston and Wichita Falls. Galveston had been devastated just a few years earlier by the massive 1900 storm that killed at least six thousand people, left another eight thousand homeless, and still stands as the deadliest natural disaster in American history.[87]

Merris's card from Wichita Falls depicted the roundhouse and railroad yards of the Fort Worth and Denver City Railway Company. The arrival of the railroad in the 1880s had transformed Wichita Falls from a loose collection of northeastern Texas shanties to a thriving market center. Ranchers were able to ship their cattle to Fort Worth, and farmers to market their products to national outlets.[88] The forceful, industrial heft of the railroad yards is evident in the postcard.

While still in Texas, the Richards & Pringle's company was attacked by a mob in Big Springs (now called Big Spring), an all-white town with a "bitter feeling . . . against the negro race."

The Alamo (built 1718), San Antonio, Texas.

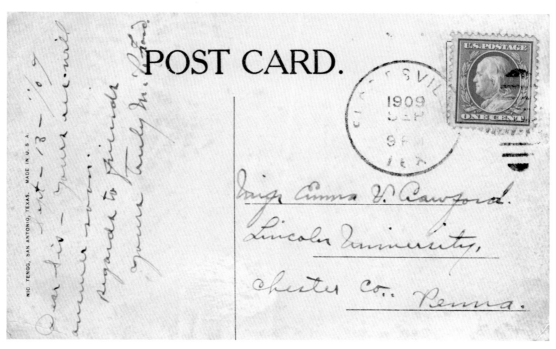

"Dear Sis—Yours rec will answer soon. Regards to friends Yours truly M.P. Ford"

Mailed in September 1909 to Emma at home. Postcard: Nic Tengg, San Antonio, Texas.

Section of Galveston Harbor, Galveston, Texas

"Will write soon. Yours truly M. P. Ford. Quanah, Texas, Oct 16, 1909. Midland, Texas, Oct 30th"

Mailed on October 4, 1909, to Emma at home. Postcard publisher: GK, New York.

Denver Round House and R.R. Yards, Wichita Falls, Tex.

"All is lovely, regards to friends. Midland Texas, Oct 30th. Yours truly, M. P. Ford"

Mailed on October 15, 1909, to Emma at home. Postcard publisher: E. [Illegible] Pub., Milwaukee, No. 6572.

NEGROES WERE MOBBED

Richard [*sic*] & Pringle's Negro Minstrels

Stormed by Mob at Big Springs Last Night

(*Herald* Special)

Big Springs, Texas, Nov. 2.—The Members of the Richard & Pringle's minstrel, all negroes, were attacked by a big mob here after the show last night and run out of town. The attack resulted from the bitter feeling here against the negro race resulting from a race riot two years ago, since which time a ban has been placed on the negro coming here. The minstrel men took refuge in their private car and were showered with bricks and other missles [*sic*], and were finally rescued by a switch engine pulling the car out of the town.[89]

Big Springs had been an all-white town since April 1907, when "all negroes not owning property were ordered to leave town in fifteen days," following the shooting death of the deputy marshal during his attempt to arrest several Black men.[90] A few weeks later, a local paper reported that all Black residents of Big Springs had been ordered out of town, not just those who weren't homeowners. The paper observed piously, "Such occurrences should be a warning to the negro race," and added, "The negroes are tolerated in many West Texas counties only under a great strain, and when they indulge in defiance of the law . . . they are told to depart and their departure promptly accelerated."[91] Racial purges of this type were not uncommon—nor were they restricted to southern states—but they were often minimized in local histories and have generally not been well documented.[92]

Given Big Springs's history, inviting an all-Black minstrel company to perform there was a questionable decision, as the events of November 2 demonstrated. It should not escape notice that the mob waited until *after* it had presumably enjoyed an evening of high-quality entertainment before it launched its attack.

Merris was among those attacked by the mob, but his cards from this period do not mention the assault. Perhaps he discussed it in letters to his mother or sister; or perhaps, because racial violence was so common, he preferred not to talk about it at all.

In the early months of 1910, Merris traveled through several southern states. In mid-March, while Emma was living with the J. Wilson Howe family, he wrote her from Thomasville, Georgia. Jones Bridge, shown in the photograph, had been erected just a few years earlier, in 1904, to traverse the Chattahoochee River. After falling into disrepair in the 1930s, the bridge ultimately collapsed in 2018.[93]

At the end of March, Merris was in Gallatin, Tennessee. His card shows the neoclassical Giles County Court House, erected the year before.

In early April, Richards & Pringle's minstrels were in Hopkinsville, Kentucky, a small tobacco town near the Tennessee border, at the beginning of a route that swung through the western part of the state before crossing into southern Illinois.[94] The card Merris sent Emma showed the then-new, sturdy brick Seventh Street School for white students, constructed in 1904–5. In contrast, Black students attended the Booker T. Washington school, a two-story wooden frame building.[95] The Seventh Street School was razed in 1974.

Later in the month, Richards & Pringle's was in Illinois. Among other buildings, Merris's card shows the University of Illinois's historic Mechanical Engineering Shop Laboratory, which had opened in 1901. The building was razed in 1992.[96]

From Illinois, Merris traveled to the upper Midwest. His final cards to Emma in 1910 were from Sioux City, Iowa, Yankton, South Dakota, and St. Cloud, Minnesota. At the turn of the century, Sioux City was a center for grain, corn, and meatpacking that prospered from railroad traffic and its location near the mouth of the Big Sioux River. The city was also notorious for its saloons, gambling dens, and houses of prostitution.[97]

Upriver of Sioux City on the Missouri River, Yankton was the historic first capital of Dakota Territory. The Yankton Theater that is shown on Merris's card opened as an opera house in 1902 and is now known as the Dakota Theatre. A contemporary ad described "Uncle Zeke," the coming attraction, as "the great laugh producing comedy. Interesting because natural. Realistic because true to life. The only rural play without a rival."

The last of Merris's 1910 cards in Emma's collection was sent from St. Cloud, in central Minnesota. With a population of about ten thousand in 1910, it was one of the larger towns he played in. The Normal School, which was the predecessor of St. Cloud State University, opened in 1869.[98]

The year 1910 was both a high point and a turning point for Black entertainers. By then minstrelsy's heyday was ending, but Tin Pan Alley, musical comedies, and vaudeville were new vehicles through which Black musicians and performers reached national audiences.[99] The transition had started nearly two decades earlier. Beginning in the 1890s, talented Black composers and lyricists had begun turning their attention to the stage, writing full-length musicals that competed with operettas and other musical shows on Broadway. Successful musical comedies staged by Black producers Cole and Johnson, Williams and Walker, and McClain

Jones' Bridge, Ocklockonee River, Thomasville, Ga.

"3–17–1910 Dear Sister, If you receive this answer at once. Yours always, Morris P. Ford. c/o Richard & Pringles Minstrels. Decatur, Ala Mar 29. Gallatin Tenn 31."

Mailed on March 17, 1910, to Emma, who was living with the Howe family in Primos, Pennsylvania. Postcard publisher: The Valentine & Sons Publishing Co., Ltd., New York.

Giles County Court House, Pulaski, Tenn.

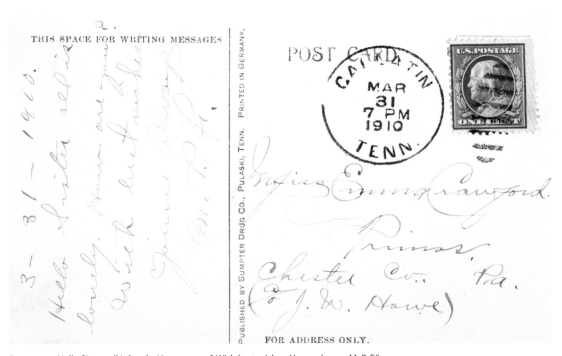

"3–31–1910 Hello Sister, all is lovely. How are you? With best wishes. Yours always, M. P. F."

Mailed on March 31, 1910, to Emma, who was living with the Howe family in Primos, Pennsylvania. Postcard publisher: Sumpter Drug Co., Pulaski, Tennessee.

7th Street School, Hopkinsville, Ky.

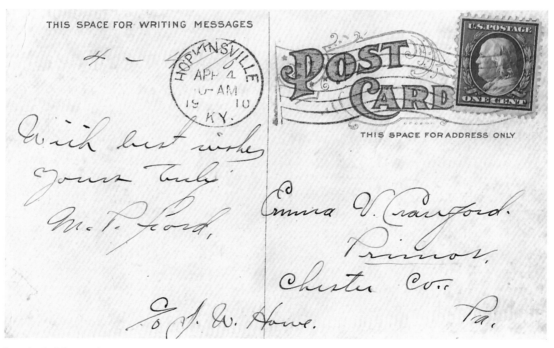

"4–4 /10 With best wishes, yours truly. M. P. Ford"

Mailed on April 4, 1910, to Emma, who was living with the Howe family in Primos, Pennsylvania. The postcard publisher is unknown (card no. #12897).

Mechanical Engineering Laboratory, Metal Shops, Electrical Laboratory, Wood Shops and Foundry, University of Illinois

"4–21–/06. Hello Sister, yours truly, M.P.F. Madison, Wis—May 1st"

Mailed on April 21, 1910, to Emma, who was living with the Howe family in Swarthmore, Pennsylvania. Postcard publisher: E. U. Williams Photoette, Bloomington, Ill., no. 1048.

Souvenir of Sioux City Iowa.

"5–11–1910 Hello Sister, How are you? I am fine and dandy. With best wishes. Yours always, M. P. Ford"

Mailed on May 12, 1910, to Emma, who was living with the Howe family in Swarthmore, Pennsylvania. Postcard publisher: H.H. & M., Sioux City, Iowa.

Yankton Theatre, Yankton, S.D.

"5–13–1910. Hello, Sister. How are you? All here is fine and dandy. With best wishes. Yours [illegible], M. P. F."

Mailed on May 13, 1910, to Emma, who was living with the Howe family in Swarthmore, Pennsylvania. Postcard publisher: N.N. 860/4.

St. Cloud Normal School, St. Cloud, Minn.

"5–26–1910. Hello, Sister. Why haven't you wrote. Hoping to hear from you in the near future. I am your affectionate Bro, Morris P. Ford."

Mailed on May 26, 1910, to Emma, who was living with the Howe family in Swarthmore, Pennsylvania. Postcard publisher: P.J. Thelsen, St. Cloud, MN, No. 2225.

Merris Porter Crawford in later life.

and Hogan played to large audiences on Broadway and in many of the first-class theaters across the nation. Elaborately staged and costumed, these productions featured the country's top Black talent.[100]

As successful as these musical comedies were, however, they could not replace minstrel shows as employers. With the decline of minstrelsy, there were fewer employment opportunities for Black entertainers, and many were forced into early retirement. But in the forty-five years since the first troupe of ex-slaves performed under the banner of Charles B. Hicks's Georgia Minstrels, it had been a strong showing for Black performers. As musical historian Henry T. Sampson recalled, "Starting out at the bottom of the political, economic, and educational ladder, blacks had successfully entered the entertainment business, bringing with them much that was new in song, dance and music which made a unique and very important contribution to American culture and . . . was seen, heard and enjoyed throughout the world."[101]

Chapter Six

Struggling and Striving

BLAZE, with your serried columns! I will not bend the knee;
The shackle ne'er again shall bind the arm which now is free
—G. W. Patten, *The Seminole's Defiance*

Like the refracted images of a kaleidoscope, Emma's postcard collection reveals many dimensions of the Crawford family's life at the start of the twentieth century: the round of work for mother, sons, and Emma; the surrounding circle of friends and extended family; the influence of Lincoln University; connections through employers with the white world. And, assembling these insights, we have some answers to the question of how Black Americans maintained a sense of agency and integrity in the face of what Frederick Douglass termed "the tide of malignant prejudice."[1] In the case of the Crawfords, simple literacy was an important advantage, giving them the tools and competencies to operate in their own behalf in the wider world. Meanwhile, their identification with the "respectable" Black middle class served as a guidepost for normative behavior. Additional strengths were their membership in religious communities and their sense of, and respect for, their own history. Their experience confirms the historic importance of three things—religious beliefs, kin networks, and education—for Black families' stability and social achievement.[2]

This chapter tells the story of the Crawfords, from their early years in postcolonial Pennsylvania until the time of Emma's postcard album. It is their unique history but also representative of the values and strategies that have been fundamental to Black families' survival across generations. Because probing the Black past is so difficult—family trees and oral histories often end at slavery's brick wall—we have too few examples of this dimension of Black American history.[3] The Crawfords' story, which I learned as oral history and have reconstructed with extensive archival research, fills in some of the gaps.

Some aspects of the territory we are about to explore are new ground that has not been well documented before. To begin with, the Crawfords were a rural family. In contrast to Philadelphia, where the large and vibrant free Black community was "the cultural and intellectual center of black America" at the beginning of the nineteenth century, there are many fewer sources of information about rural Black life in Pennsylvania.[4] Philadelphia's Black social infrastructure was robust and included churches, charitable organizations, mutual aid groups, insurance companies, libraries, loan associations, and schools—all in some way associated with a documentary record.[5] There was much less infrastructure in rural areas, where Black populations were small and scattered, and formal records were scarce.[6]

The widespread omission of Black people from official nineteenth-century records adds to the research challenge. In Pennsylvania local directories and atlases tended to exclude or purposely obscure data on African Americans.[7] Meanwhile, in the federal decennial census, Black families might appear in one census record but not a decade later (or earlier). Census details like occupation and literacy might be left blank for Black households while being meticulously recorded for each member of white households.

In nineteenth- and early twentieth-century newspapers, human-interest items about the smallest details of whites' daily lives were commonplace, but Black people were rarely mentioned other than as subjects of comedic observation, derision, or criminal suspicion. With extraordinary candor a white editor acknowledged in 1908, "We hold [Black people] up to ridicule, we show, humorously, their dense ignorance and quaint views to make white folks laugh, and we tell with unfailing regularity of the worst they are guilty of, not forgetting to say 'big black brute' and narrate how he was lynched."[8] For Chester County, the situation improved somewhat in the later decades of the nineteenth century, when correspondents for Black newspapers like the *Indianapolis Freeman* or the *Broad Axe* (St. Paul) reported from time to time on local events, although their focus was usually on Lincoln University and its graduates.

Thus, Black Pennsylvanians were underrepresented in the official record as Americans worthy of respect and official documentation. Consequently, understanding the dimensions of family and community life requires determined effort and the weaving together of snippets and hints of information derived from many sources.

Proctors and Fords

The earliest history of the Crawfords awaits documentation. I do not yet know when their progenitors arrived in the New World from Africa (and Europe; like many African Americans, they were of racially mixed ancestry) or how long they were enslaved. Their known history begins two generations before Emma's birth, in the early 1800s, when a free Black man named James Proctor and his wife, Hannah Frisco Proctor, settled in southern Lancaster County's Drumore Township, just a few miles north of the Maryland border. James was born "before 1775" (in the terminology of the 1820 census) and Hannah in 1782. Both were native Pennsylvanians who were either born free or had been manumitted at an early age.

Slavery in Pennsylvania dated to the first years of European settlement, in the 1630s.[9] Initially it was more prevalent in colonial Philadelphia than in rural communities, but around the mid-eighteenth century slavery in rural Pennsylvania became more common, spreading to Chester, Lancaster, and other southeastern counties, where Emma Crawford's forebears lived.[10] However, most labor needs in these counties—and the colony as a whole—continued to be filled by free labor, provided either by white farmers, their families, or apprentices and hired laborers.[11]

Because of this preference for free labor, in combination with a climate that did not support large-scale agrarian labor, the number of enslaved Black people remained small relative to Pennsylvania's total population. For example, in 1790, the year of the first federal census, enslaved Black people were less than 1 percent of the state's population, while there were nearly twice as many "free non-white people." In every southern state, on the other hand—except for Delaware and Kentucky—slaves were at least 25 percent of the population, and the number of free nonwhite people was minuscule.[12]

But even though their numbers were not large, enslaved African Americans were an integral part of Pennsylvania's early development. Black men worked in a variety of settings, including fields, mills, and forges. Some had skills such as masonry, sugar making, coopering (making barrels), and tanning leather.[13] Black women cooked, cleaned, washed and ironed laundry, kept fires, gardened, helped with children, and served as maids. In rural communities they also tended gardens, raised poultry, milked cows, wove cloth, and helped in the fields.[14] One nostalgic history reported, "Every family of any size had at least two [slaves]," adding without irony, "and the routine of domestic life moved along much more smoothly than at the present time."[15]

In 1780 the passage of the Gradual Abolition Act initiated the emancipation of Pennsylvania's enslaved Black residents decades before the Emancipation Proclamation and Thirteenth Amendment officially ended US slavery in the 1860s. Fueled by the revolutionary spirit that accompanied the Declaration of Independence, the Gradual Abolition Act was designed to end slavery by establishing a formal transition to indentured servitude. Under its provisions, Black children born after March 1, 1780, were registered as indentured servants until they reached twenty-eight years of age, when they would be considered free. Meanwhile, Black people who had been enslaved before March 1, 1780, could be registered as slaves for life. About six thousand people fell into this latter category.

While the abolition of slavery was gradual, the 1780 Act lifted restrictive laws on free Black people at once, giving them the same rights as whites except for the ability to serve in the state militia and—most critical as American citizens—the right to vote.[16] Pennsylvania's Black males did not gain the right to vote until 1870, when the Fourteenth Amendment of the United States Constitution was ratified (Black women's voting rights were delayed until the passage of the Nineteenth Amendment in 1920).[17]

In James and Hannah Proctor's time, free and enslaved Black people accounted for perhaps 2 percent of Lancaster County's population. As more members of the Black population were freed, they established small enclaves and attempted to develop a community life. However, white resistance to African American land ownership made economic independence nearly impossible in an agricultural economy. As a result, most Black farm workers were "cottagers," that is, landless workers akin to indentured servants. Others were meagerly paid agricultural day laborers or tenant farmers.[18]

James Proctor's social and financial status was unquestionably precarious, but there are signs that where possible he participated in broader community life. For example, he married Hannah in 1802 at Trinity Lutheran Church, a mainstream white church in Lancaster City, and he baptized one of his sons there. In his forties James Proctor owned a plot of land and was one of a small group of Black men who achieved landowner status. His location may have provided some form of advantage, because both Drumore Township and nearby Little Britain Township were noteworthy for their Black property ownership.[19]

One of James and Hannah Proctor's several children was a daughter Maria (pronounced "Mariah"), born in 1822. As an adult Maria was respected as a "ghost breaker"—someone who could remove hexes from the farms and houses of Lancaster County farmers. I wish I knew more about how she developed this reputation. Maybe Black women were generally believed to have magical powers—I'm thinking here of how Emma's mother, Isabella, was once called on to remove a spell from someone's house, and of Emma's aunt who read tea leaves—or perhaps Maria had demonstrated specific abilities. My research into this question is ongoing.

Maria was also known to be fearless. In my childhood I heard many times from my mother how she "walked the lonely roads of Lancaster County with just a knife in her boot, fearing neither man nor beast."

Maria Proctor Ford, 1822–1908.

"She walked the lonely roads of Lancaster County with just a knife in her boot, fearing neither man nor beast."

Considering the proximity of southern Lancaster County to the Mason-Dixon Line, and the risk of being kidnapped by ruthless men who captured free Blacks and sold them across the line, Maria's fearlessness is truly remarkable.

When she was about seventeen, Maria married a free Black man named John Ford, from Chester County, who was born in 1819. John and Maria's story, building on that of their parents, reflects the evolution of Black life in Pennsylvania during the middle decades of the nineteenth century.

Establishing a social and economic foothold was no easier for John and Maria Ford than it had been for their parents. Mid-century economic changes in the state, compounded by waves of newly arrived German and Irish immigrants and deepening racism and discrimination, resulted in a narrowing of options for Black men who were looking for steady and racially equitable employment.[20] Increasingly, over the course of the century, writes historian Douglas Harper, Pennsylvania's Black workers were "'excluded from the most respectable and profitable employments of life, confined to the humblest and least gainful occupations.' They were being squeezed out by petition and organized white labor action from even the most menial jobs. [For example,] by 1824, the 'prejudice and pride' of white competitors had effectively excluded Blacks in Pennsylvania from turnpikes, canals, coal mines, brick-making, street-paving, and even from the occasional work of shoveling snow from Philadelphia's cobblestone streets."[21] Broadly speaking, white workers opposed any efforts to have Black people as fellow workers.[22]

These obstacles may have been what led John to leave Pennsylvania for New Bedford, Massachusetts, where he was employed for a time on a whaling ship. In the early part of the nineteenth century, New Bedford was prosperous, cosmopolitan, and a refuge for urban Black men, escaped formerly enslaved men, young immigrants, former city factory laborers, and rural farmhands.[23] Work was abundant on the city's whalers, and in its shipyards, shops, and factories.[24] More than three thousand African American men signed up for New Bedford whaling expeditions between 1800 and 1860. There was generally less discrimination than in land-bound jobs, and pay was racially equitable for comparable jobs.[25] Because the cash wages were a potential source of capital accumulation, Black families were proud to have a whaling son.[26]

In the 1830s, however, the situation began to change. Gradually, fewer Black men were employed on whalers. During the 1840s there was an average of two per vessel, but by the 1850s it was one or none. Increasingly, African American whaling men were given less favored positions, because of competition from white immigrants and rising racism in reaction to the pre–Civil War debate about slavery. This gradual shift in attitudes, along with the reduced availability of work, may have been what brought John Ford back to Lancaster County. In the 1850s he settled with Maria and their children in Fulton Township, where he worked as a farm laborer.

Fulton Township was the southernmost part of Lancaster County, close to the Pennsylvania-Maryland border and to the Mason-Dixon Line, which, after 1781, was the demarcation between slave and free states.[27] Crossed by numerous paths of the Underground Railroad, the area was the scene of many conflicts between enslaved men and women, slave catchers, and abolitionists. It was also one of five townships in southern Lancaster County that in the mid-nineteenth century had a sizable (for rural Pennsylvania) free Black population. In 1850 there were 277 African Americans in Fulton Township, 321 in Drumore Township (where Maria Proctor Ford had grown up), 140 in Martic Township, 148 in Sadsbury Township, and 239 in Little Britain Township. By comparison, the free Black community in Philadelphia, about eighty miles away, numbered around twenty thousand people.

Whereas southern Black people who lived on plantations with large enslaved populations had enough numbers to sustain many African linguistic, religious, and cultural practices, Lancaster County's Black population was too small and scattered for this. Instead, living and working in proximity to whites—although excluded from mainstream institutions—they absorbed the prevailing culture and modified it to suit their purposes. Their religious life is one example of this adaptive process.

In the first decades of the nineteenth century, Lancaster County's Black population worshipped in the churches of the majority community and were members of leading local churches, like St. James Episcopal and Trinity Lutheran.[28] After whites began systematically excluding Black worshippers from congregations, Black community members organized their own religious bodies—just as they had done in Philadelphia a few decades earlier, thereby establishing America's first Black churches.[29] By 1850 there were at least ten African American congregations in Lancaster County, including three in Fulton Township: the Asbury African Methodist Episcopal Church, active from 1844; the Mount Sinai Union American Methodist Episcopal Church, active from 1837 (and still in existence); and the Rigby Union American Methodist Episcopal Church, active from 1837.[30]

Maria Ford's brother Jeremiah Proctor was one of two local ministers at Asbury African Methodist Church. The church was: "a log structure, one-story in height, twenty-five by twenty feet in its dimensions . . . erected about the year 1842, and named Asbury, in the honor of Francis Asbury, the abolitionist and second Bishop of the Methodist Episcopal Church (white) in America. The money to erect this building was collected by subscriptions. At the time this house was built, or soon afterwards, the congregation consisted of sixty-eight members."[31]

Although small, Asbury African Methodist and its sister churches played a crucial role in the survival of Lancaster County's Black community. They served many functions in addition to spiritual guidance: as incubators of Black leadership and antislavery advocacy; as schools, social outlets, sources of mutual aid, and protection against a hostile larger society; and as stations on the Underground Railroad.[32] Above all, actively contradicting everything congregants experienced outside church walls, religious leaders ceaselessly insisted that the equality of all people, regardless of race, was a bedrock of Christianity, "the religion of that beneficent Parent, who has made of one blood all nations of men who dwell upon the face of the whole earth."[33] Thus, churches fortified Black Americans' hopes for social equality and communicated the unshakable understanding that racism was both a corruption of Christian ideals and a betrayal of the spirit of the nation's founding. In the words of Rev. Peter Williams, "No people in the world profess so high a respect for liberty and equality as the people of the United States, and yet no people hold so many slaves, or make such great distinctions between man and man."[34]

At a cultural level, churches enabled Black northerners to maintain African traditions of exuberant religious expression within a Christian framework. In 1834 the German scholar Francis Lieber wrote, "Some years ago I went into one of the principal Methodist meeting-houses of coloured people in Philadelphia, and I never shall forget the impression made upon me by the unbounded excitement and passion of the congregation."[35] In a similar vein, Fredrika Bremer wrote in 1850, of an African Methodist Church in Cincinnati, Ohio:

> I found in the African Church African ardor and African life. The church was full to overflowing, and the congregation sang their own hymns. The singing ascended and poured forth like a melodious torrent, and the heads, feet and elbows of the congregation moved all in unison with it, amid evident enchantment and delight in the singing . . .
>
> The hymns and psalms which the negroes have themselves composed have a peculiar *naïve* character, childlike, full of imagery and life.[36]

Thus, the Black Church, while outwardly modeled on and resembling other northern churches, acted as the guardian of African cultural content and values. It also served as the bedrock of an evolving Black community infrastructure. For, as historian Edward Turner observed, "in spite of all obstacles there had begun to appear negroes who owned their houses, paid taxes, supported their own schools, contributed to beneficial societies, built churches, and constituted not only a negro population but a negro society."[37]

By 1860 several of John and Maria Ford's older children were no longer living at home. Still teenagers, they were recorded in that year's census as living with white families as domestic servants or farm laborers, or as boarding in the households of other African Americans. In northern cities, a sizable proportion of Black adults boarded with other Black families.[38] The Ford children's experience suggests that this was true in rural communities as well. In 1859 John Ford lay ill with heart disease in the segregated section of the Chester County Poorhouse. Boarding the older Ford children with relatives would have been a way of coping with the economic hardship posed by his illness—and likely death—and of providing a source of social support. Four Ford children were still at home in 1860, living with Maria and their widowed grandmother Hannah Proctor.

Isabella, Emma Crawford's mother, was one of the Ford children who left home at a young age. In 1860, at age twelve, she boarded with relatives to attend school—probably a segregated "African" school—in the

Quarryville section of Lancaster County. This was an important step in her development that reflected not only the enduring value that the Black community placed on education for women and men alike but also the Ford family's ability—and willingness—to invest in a child who could otherwise have contributed to the family's resources as an unschooled domestic or farm worker.[39] The economic sacrifice entailed by the Ford family's decision was recouped in Isabella's lifetime by the worldview and exposure that literacy provided her—which ultimately bore fruit in a multigenerational family commitment to educational advancement.

In 1818 Prince Saunders had urged the Pennsylvania Augustine Society for the Education of People of Colour, "Let it be the unceasing labour, the undeviating and the inflexibly firm purpose of the members of this Association—individually and collectively—to inspire all within the sphere of their influence with a sense of the value and importance of giving their children a good education."[40] Thirty years later the Quakers lent their weight to this cause, asserting in an 1847 study of Black Philadelphia, "There is no way in which the patriotic man of colour can so promote the well-being of his people, as in kindling and keeping alive the desire for instruction."[41] And in an 1853 letter to Harriet Beecher Stowe, Frederick Douglass identified ignorance, along with poverty and degradation, as "the social disease of the Free Colored people in the United States."[42] The Ford family would have shared Douglass's commitment to fighting these threats, using all of the means available to them.

Before the desegregation of Pennsylvania's public schools in the 1880s (by law if not always in practice), Black families that wished to educate their children usually turned to privately financed African schools. A system of public education had been established by the Pennsylvania legislature in 1834, but Black children's access to these schools was ambiguously neither guaranteed nor denied. A measure passed in 1854 essentially established segregated schools by permitting the comptrollers and directors of the state's school districts to establish separate schools for Black children wherever they could accommodate twenty or more pupils. Meanwhile, another provision stipulated that wherever Black schools were established, directors and comptrollers were not compelled to admit Black pupils to any other schools of that district. In practice, the law was interpreted to mean that Black and white children could attend school together only when no Black school was available.[43]

It is unclear which of the segregated schools Isabella attended, but Lancaster County was dotted with several. Of the African school located in Lancaster City, an 1849 report noted that "children of every age and of both sexes are there taught. . . . The pupils of this school have made great progress in their studies, and if they possessed the advantages enjoyed by white children, of being transferred to higher schools as they advanced in their studies, would undoubtedly become good scholars."[44]

Isabella matriculated from the eighth grade, the upper standard for the day, and studied a curriculum that included Latin, and probably, history, grammar, geography, and arithmetic. For her day, when it was illegal to educate enslaved Black people and northern Black children were not guaranteed schooling, she was exceptionally well educated, especially for a Black woman. Even among whites, only about half of all five- to nineteen year-olds were enrolled in school during this period.[45] Isabella's educational advantages notwithstanding, the only employment open to her throughout her adult life was as a domestic. Undoubtedly, she was often as educated as the white women she worked for—or more so. Her ability to tolerate the employment she was forced into without losing interest in more-intellectual pursuits is testimony to her personal commitment to pursuing her goals, and to the collective Black values that undergirded that commitment.

In contrast to Isabella's education stood her brother Jeremiah's. In 1864, when Jeremiah Ford enlisted in Company A of the Twenty-Fifth Regiment of the United States Colored Troops (USCT), he signed his papers with an X, suggesting that he was illiterate or perhaps had been taught to read but not to write (e.g., at a church-based school where the focus was on reading the Scriptures).[46] Why Isabella enjoyed more educational advantages than her brother is a mystery, but it may have been that the family's need for his wages as a laborer overwhelmed other considerations.

After entering the USCT as a private, Jeremiah was promoted to corporal later that year and saw action in North Carolina and New Orleans, before mustering out in 1865.[47] His older brother, John Ford Jr., was a private in Company C of the Third Regiment of the USCT, which was active in South Carolina and Florida.[48] Together, they were among 8,612 free Black Pennsylvanians who fought for the Union, perhaps motivated to sign up by Frederick Douglass's passionate speeches and writings urging engagement in the war as a moral duty that united Black and white males in a common purpose and confirmed Black males' entitlement to equal civil rights.[49]

> If you are sound in body and mind, there is nothing in your *color* to excuse you from enlisting in the service of the republic against its enemies. If *color* should not be a criterion of rights, neither should it be a standard of duty. The whole duty of a man, belongs alike to white and black.[50]

❖ ❖ ❖

In 1870, at age twenty-two, Isabella Ford moved from Lancaster County to Concord Township in Delaware County, close to the Pennsylvania-Delaware border. She boarded there with the Fairfax family, who were described in the census as former slaves, and took her first job as a domestic servant. All women of the era were limited in their occupational options, but for Black women the limitations were severe. The work available to them was essentially unchanged from a century earlier. In cities Black women were washerwomen, seamstresses, cooks, domestics, schoolmistresses, shopkeepers, and keepers of boarding, eating, and oyster houses. In rural Pennsylvania they most likely worked as cooks, washerwomen, nannies, and general domestics. Rural women probably boarded with nearby Black families, as Isabella did, or lived in the servants' quarters of white households, as she and her daughter Emma did in later years.

Crawfords

While living in Delaware County, Isabella met Joseph Crawford, the son of free "mulattos" (as they were described in the 1850 census) who had moved to Pennsylvania from the state of Delaware sometime in the early 1830s. Historically, Delaware's enslaved Black population was larger than those of any of the northern states, although smaller than those in any of the southern states. Enslaved Black people made up 20 to 25 percent of the total population in the decade prior to the American Revolution, falling to 15 percent of the population at the time of the 1790 census. Because of factors that made slave owning increasingly unprofitable, most of the Black population was free by the end of the eighteenth century, making Delaware the first state in the country with a significant percentage of free African Americans. By 1840 about nine in ten of the state's African Americans were free.[51]

Following Nat Turner's 1831 rebellion in Virginia, Delaware's white population grew increasingly apprehensive of free Black people, fearing that they not only were less docile than they had previously believed but were potentially more dangerous than enslaved people. This led to the imposition in the early 1830s of a series of "Black codes," which, notes historian William Williams, were "designed to degrade, to crush and to render [Blacks] ignorant and powerless."[52] The codes reduced Black residents to a degrading limbo that was neither slave nor free. In response to these deteriorating conditions—paired with the continuing danger of being kidnapped and sold as slaves into the Deep South—many free Black people left the state for Pennsylvania, other northern states, or Canada.

James Crawford, Joseph's father, was one of the free Black people who left. Born about 1807, by the mid-1830s he had settled in Chester County, Pennsylvania. There he worked as a laborer with Rev. Josiah Philips, a Baptist minister and lime manufacturer (lime was often used at the time to improve soil quality).[53] He also did farm labor and, most significantly, founded a church in London Grove Township, near present-day Chatham, called King Solomon's Temple. Eventually the small Black settlement around the church also came to be known as Solomon's Temple.[54]

King Solomon's Temple was a congregation of the African Union Church, the oldest independent Black denomination in the United States.[55] Like the better-known African Methodist Episcopal Church, the African Union Church was organized in protest to the racism Black worshippers experienced in white Methodist churches. Chartered in 1813 by Peter Spencer, a former slave, in Wilmington, Delaware, it emphasized family and church as the twin pillars of meaningful, moral, and economically successful lives for African Americans. Members were encouraged to be honest and hardworking.[56] Church values included education, temperance, moral reform, frugality, race pride and self-help.[57]

A unique and significant feature of African Union Methodism is the annual gathering known as Big August Quarterly, held in Wilmington, Delaware, that was inaugurated by Peter Spencer in 1814 and continues to this day. First modeled, it appears, on the annual meetings of the Quakers, Big August Quarterly was Black America's first major religious festival. As a general reunion and religious revival, it attracted Black people—initially both free and enslaved—from Delaware, southeastern Pennsylvania, and the eastern shores of Maryland and Virginia. In the past, Big August Quarterly included West African religious elements like spirit possession and ring dances, as well as faith healing. Now the gathering honors Black traditions via preaching, singing, feasting, and storytelling.[58]

The stone foundations of a modest wooden building are all that remains today of King Solomon's Temple's. However, the cemetery, which is still partially intact, bears witness to the church's role as the focal point of life for the Crawford family and other free Black families in London Grove Township. The gravestones include not only those of immediate family members and members of families into which the Crawford children married but also those of nonfamily members who were part of the church community. As burial records attest, the church remained active long after James Crawford's own death.

With his wife, Martha Trusty, a free woman of mixed African American and Lenni Lenape (Delaware) Indian descent, James Crawford raised four children, three of whom lived to adulthood. His sons James and Joseph attended school in the vicinity of Cochranville, Penn Township, Chester County. Family circumstances may have compromised his daughter Sarah's education, for, as an adult, she signed papers with an X. Again, as in the example of the Ford family, access to crucial literacy skills was not equally available to family members, with consequences not only for the individual in question but also for their descendants.

◆ ◆ ◆

James H.—Emma's uncle and the elder of the Crawford sons—had a remarkable story that illustrates some of the dramatic changes in Black people's lives that were brought about by the Civil War and Reconstruction. A hostler (person who cares for horses) at age twenty, James H. (he customarily used J. H.) eventually moved to post–Civil War North Carolina, where he was active for the rest of his life as an educator, minister, and legislator. Reconstruction presented him with an extraordinary opportunity as a Black man to participate in the rebuilding of the South and the advancement of its formerly enslaved Black population.

The pivotal experience that took James H. from rural Chester County to playing a historic role in North Carolina was his enrollment at Ashmun Institute, the world's first institution for the higher education of Black men. Founded in 1854 as a Presbyterian "College and Theological Seminary for colored men," Ashmun Institute was located in a small Chester County village called Hinsonville, about ten miles from the Crawfords' home in London Grove. Like London Grove, Hinsonville was a free Black settlement with an African Union church at its nucleus, in this instance Hosanna African Union Methodist Church, founded in 1843. In 1866 Ashmun Institute was renamed Lincoln University. It became the country's first degree-granting Black university, while Hinsonville was rechristened Lincoln University, Pennsylvania.

Ashmun Institute was named for Reverend Jehudi Ashmun, one of the agents of the American Colonization Society, an early nineteenth-century organization that brought together abolitionists who believed Black Americans would face better chances for freedom in Africa than in the United States with slaveholders who saw repatriation as a way to remove free Black people from slave societies. The Society secured land in West Africa and established the colony of Liberia, where they wanted freed people to settle.[59] The Ashmun Institute was founded with the associated goal of training African American missionaries for service in Liberia and other colonies.[60]

Most free Black men and women, proudly identifying as native-born Americans, were viscerally opposed to the goals of the American Colonization Society. "We have no wish to separate from our present homes for any purpose whatever," Philadelphia sailmaker James Forten wrote in 1817.[61] A decade later David Walker's *Appeal*, quoting Richard Allen, founder of the African Methodist Episcopal Church, said, "This land which we have watered with our *tears* and *our blood*, is now our *mother country*, and we are well satisfied to stay."[62] The Black perspective, as historian Richard R. Wright Jr. describes, was that "the American Colonization Society was an organized expression of the sentiment that Negroes could not assimilate with whites and had no future in this country except that of slaves . . . It told the Negroes that their only hope was in Africa."[63]

James H. may have shared this attitude, because in 1865, after completing a course of studies at Ashmun that included theology, metaphysics, Greek, and Latin, and being ordained by the Institute as a Presbyterian minister, he chose post–Civil War North Carolina for his mission, rather than West Africa.[64] The opportunity to help his own people and to fill the need for teachers in the newly emancipated South was powerfully compelling.

During Reconstruction, thousands of Black and white teachers from the North and South responded to the "overwhelming surge toward the school-house door" of the newly freed slaves. Contrary to the popular image of these teachers as white women from New England, between 1861 and 1876 Black teachers from northern and southern states outnumbered northern white teachers by a ratio of four to three.[65] Like James H. Crawford, some of the northern Black teachers had attended or graduated college; others had attended a normal school or preparatory school. Collectively, these more educated teachers constituted a "small but remarkable" group within the larger mass of Black teachers who, for the most part, had, as historian Ronald Butchart has written, "the rough equivalent of a common school education or, often, much less."[66]

Under the sponsorship of the Presbyterian Church, James H. established schools in several North Carolina communities, including Franklinton, Oxford, Warrenton, and Louisburg. Franklinton's Albion Academy, which educated generations of Black students until it closed in 1933, evolved out of one of James H.'s schools.[67] The challenges he faced making the adjustment from Chester County's small but established Black communities to living among the newly freed, penniless formerly enslaved people and other survivors of the devastating war must have been immense.

James H. brought a sense of mission to his work that was widely noted, as were his exceptional skills as an educator and a minister.[68]

[May 5, 1866]

. . . This school (Freedmen's School) is one of the best in the State. It is taught by J. H. Crawford, who is an excellent teacher, and who also knows well how to preach the gospel. He told me that he had sixty four scholars.

When this house was first talked of, the people of Franklinton did not want it. Some said:

"Just to think of the idea of a negro school being here!" But now they have altered their minds. All who count themselves either ladies or gentlemen, say that it is the greatest thing that ever has been in this section of the country."

. . .

Respectfully yours,
Pattie J. Jones[69]

[March 11, 1866]

. . . We left Raleigh on Thursday, the 15th, with great reluctance, but at the call of duty, for a little place called Frankleton [*sic*]. We arrived there a little after six o-clock, and were met by Mr. W. H. Bookram, an old citizen, and Rev. Mr. Crawford, the teacher of the school at that place. . . . We visited Mr. Crawford's school, and we are delighted to say that we found it in a highly flourishing condition, which reflects great credit upon its talented teacher. Mr. Crawford is one of our best young men. In intelligence, perseverance, and gentlemanly deportment, he has few equals. He is a pupil of Ashmun. His school is composed of persons of both sexes and all ages—children, young ladies, young men, and married people. A more interesting set of pupils we have seldom met with, and their deep earnestness and great anxiety to learn is very cheering to all interested in the intellectual development of our race.[70]

James H.'s letters to the Freedmen's Bureau and the African American newspaper the *Christian Recorder* poignantly captured both the enthusiastic response of the newly freed slaves to the Presbyterian schools and the challenges for the poor, both Black and white, in the war-torn state.[71] In one, he sharply questioned the administration of justice in post-Emancipation North Carolina:

For the Christian Recorder.
North Carolina Correspondence.
Franklinton, N.C., April 7, 1866.

Mr. Editor:

. . . I will close this letter with a few remarks concerning the treatment of our people by the civil law.

Whipping-Posts in Raleigh

With much pain I inform you that several colored persons, for the crime of larceny, have been punished with whipping, in Raleigh and one in this place.

Now, if this is the law of the State, what is the use of our toiling as we are now, and as we have been doing for the last four years. We left our homes to save our country, but we learned that the chains of slavery had to be cut before our country could be saved. As we entered each town, we cut down the whipping-posts immediately. Through chilling storms we marched to destroy those posts; but of what use, we ask, was our toil, if negroes are still to be whipped? Is it religiously or morally right for us, as men who have suffered so much for their country, to allow such brutal conduct to escape our notice? Yours forever, with great respect,

J. H. Crawford[72]

Opposition to James H.'s reforms by the mayor of Franklinton and other white residents came to a head in an 1866 effort to remove him from his position as a teacher and minister on the grounds that "a certain series of religious meetings which he held two consecutive evenings . . . were noisy, protracted to unusually later hours, and demoralizing in their effects upon the Freedmen." In response, F. A. Fiske, superintendent of education for the North Carolina Bureau of Refugees, Freedmen, and Abandoned Lands, met with "more than a hundred Freedmen" who attested to James H.'s "good habits and good morals." Fiske concluded that "it would be injust to Mr. Crawford [and] injurious to the educational interests of the Freedmen in Franklinton . . . to remove Mr. Crawford."[73] A year later, James H. was named Superintendent of Schools for Franklinton and the neighboring towns of Oxford, Warrenton, and Louisburg.

During Reconstruction, James H. achieved statewide influence as an 1869–70 member of the North Carolina House of Representatives (R-Granville), one of three representatives from that county.[74] The Republicans dominated the state government and oversaw the drafting of a

Joseph Taylor Crawford, 1851–1920.

new, more democratic, state constitution that included creation of the state's first functioning public school system, affirmation of the legal and political equality of the races, and steps to alleviate economic distress in the population.[75] These advancements stood until the mid-1870s, when the reestablishment of white supremacy reversed the gains of Reconstruction.[76] In his later years, James H. remained active and established several congregations, most notably the Second Presbyterian Church of Mocksville, North Carolina.[77]

◆ ◆ ◆

Joseph Taylor Crawford, Emma's father, took a different path from his older brother James H. that illustrates some of the options available in the second half of the nineteenth century for a literate, rural Black man. A lifelong resident of Chester County, Joseph's preferred line of work was public speaking, referred to at the time as "declaiming." I do not know how his interest in oratory developed, but mid-nineteenth-century African American literary societies, such as Philadelphia's Reading Room Society for Men of Color, promoted vocal expression, and it's possible that a local gathering of this type encouraged him. Organized for both men and women, Black literary societies aspired to improve and elevate the condition of African Americans by providing settings for shared knowledge and intellectual development.[78] They viewed reading, writing, and speaking skills as vital elements of educating individuals who would consider themselves to be capable, respected citizens.[79]

As a declaimer, Joseph was employed during some periods on excursion boats that toured on the scenic Delaware Water Gap in northeastern Pennsylvania. His signature poem was "The Seminole's Defiance," described by its white author, G. W. Patten, as the imagined sentiments of "the indomitable Seminole chief Osceola who was captured by treachery while conferring under a flag of truce and whose proud defiant spirit remained unconquered through cruel imprisonment even unto death."[80] The circumstances of Osceola's 1837 capture caused a national uproar, and he was subsequently buried with military honors at Fort Moultrie in South Carolina.[81] Thus, in his day he was a sympathetic figure—in striking contrast to the likely public perception of any African American man who dared to similarly challenge white authority.

The Seminole's Defiance

Blaze, with your serried columns! I will not bend the knee;
The shackle ne'er again shall bind the arm which now is free!
I've mailed it with the thunder, when the tempest muttered low;
And where it falls, ye well may dread the lightning of its blow
I've scared you in the city; I've scalped you on the plain;
Go, count your chosen where they fell beneath my leaden rain!
I scorn your proffered treaty; the pale face I defy;
Revenge is stamped upon my spear, and "blood" my battle cry!

Some strike for hope of booty; some to defend their all:—
I battle for the joy I have to see the white man fall.
I love, among the wounded, to hear his dying moan,
And catch, while chanting at his side, the music of his groan.
Ye've trailed me through the forest; ye've tracked me o'er the stream;
And struggling through the everglade your bristling bayonets gleam.
But I stand as should the warrior, with his rifle and his spear; The
scalp of vengeance still is red, and warns you—"Come not here!"

Think ye to find my homestead?—I gave it to the fire.
My tawny household do ye seek?—I am a childless sire. But, should
ye crave life's nourishment, enough I have, and good;
I live on hate—'t is all my bread; yet light is not my food.

I loathe you with my bosom! I scorn you with mine eye!
And I'll taunt you with my latest breath, and fight you till I die!
I ne'er will ask for quarter, and I ne'er will be your slave;
But I'll swim the sea of slaughter till I sink beneath its wave![82]

As a passionate statement of racial defiance, "The Seminole's Defiance" enabled Joseph to express a powerful criticism of white aggression in the guise of Osceola's voice, a criticism that perhaps reflected his own feelings as a man of mixed American Indian and African American heritage. The fact that the poem was popular among white declaimers would have helped mask any personal meaning it held for him.

Generally speaking, mid-nineteenth-century Black tradesmen were more successful when their work could be done at home or in other settings that didn't bring them into close contact with prejudiced white laborers.[83] Following this pattern, Joseph was a barber and shoemaker—tasks that could be performed independently—in addition to his seasonal work as a declaimer. Barbering was a respected profession that African American men had dominated for decades in Philadelphia, often serving a racially mixed clientele.[84] Meanwhile, most of his rural peers were farm laborers or domestic workers.[85] This was especially true after the Civil War, when unschooled former slaves began moving to Pennsylvania in large numbers.

Writing of this mid-century period from the vantage point of 1899, Du Bois observed: "In the half century 1840 to 1890 the proportion of Negroes who are domestic servants has not greatly changed; the mass of the remainder are still laborers; their opportunities for employment have been restricted by three causes: competition, industrial change, color prejudice."[86] Of the period's racial prejudice in particular, Black Philadelphian Joseph Willson wrote in 1841, "The exceedingly illiberal, unjust and oppressive prejudices of the great mass of the white community . . . is enough to crush—effectually crush and keep down—any people."[87]

In the face of these dynamics, Joseph's literacy gave him a clear occupational and economic advantage relative to the mass of Black working men. He was able to pursue lines of work in which he could develop unique skills, and he was sheltered to some extent from the industrial advances that reduced opportunities for manual laborers and agricultural workers. In the process his ability to maintain a stable family life and to transmit his cultural and educational values to his children was also reinforced. His values were no doubt shaped by the African Union church's focus on family and religion, along with the frequently expressed sentiment within the free Black community that individuals should act for the good of the race and "pass on to coming generations the practical tools of progress, that is, education and skills, knowledge and property."[88]

In 1873 Joseph Crawford and Isabella Ford married. At the time, most American households, both Black and white, were headed by married couples, even though the severe socioeconomic pressures that African Americans experienced made it difficult for them to maintain stable two-parent families.[89] During the 1880s the couple moved with their children from the Penn/New Garden Township area of Chester County to Lower Oxford Township, settling in the historically Black village that was on the outskirts of Lincoln University.

Lincoln University's faculty and trustees were all white at the time, while the all-male Black student body was a geographically diverse mix representing northern and southern states, the Caribbean, and Africa.[90] Living in proximity to this small but dynamic, education-oriented community presented new experiences for the family that were of lasting significance. Faculty members were sources of employment for both Isabella and Emma. Meanwhile, taking advantage of the university's public lectures and concerts, family members were exposed to the country's first generations of Black academics and theologians. The university was an atmosphere of "a high level of decorum," where men who "had learned all of their lives the bitter lessons of an enforced inferiority . . . would develop the habit of thinking of themselves as men."[91] Thus, in stark contrast to the larger society, it was a setting of white-supported Black achievement in which family and racial values of intellectual development, self-improvement, morality, and respectability were affirmed and reinforced.

In their relationship with the university, family members developed sustained ties with some of the white faculty that rose above the usual employer-employee relationship. These ties were not only a means for expanding the family's world; they were also a source of allies for dealing with the segregated world outside the university enclave. For example, one such association, with the Finney family, no doubt started as a work relationship but appears to have turned into a decades-long friendship, based on the trail of postcards spanning from 1906 to 1927. Rev. William P. Finney was a professor of English literature at the university and a cousin of its founder, John Miller Dickey.[92]

◆ ◆ ◆

Isabella and Joseph Crawford eventually had five children—Jerry, Merris Porter, William Fulton, Philip Bushong, and Emma Victoria—who, coming of age in the decades just before and after the beginning of the twentieth century, are some of the people with whom our story started.

Looking back to their great-grandparents' childhoods in the newly independent United States, the Crawford children would certainly have

Famous Old Landmark – the Elephant at South Atlantic City.

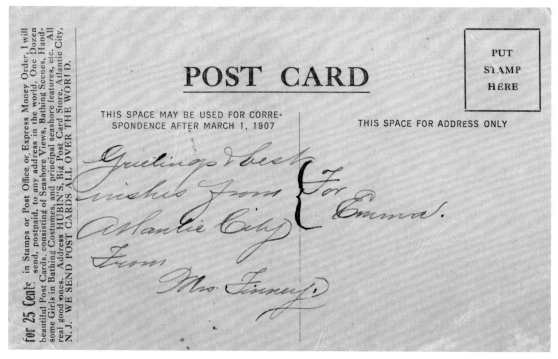

"For Emma. Greetings and best wishes from Atlantic City. From Mrs. Finney."

An unmailed card, circa 1906. Postcard publisher: Hubin's Big Post Card Store, Atlantic City, New Jersey.

Greetings from Atlantic City. Greetings from the Seaside.

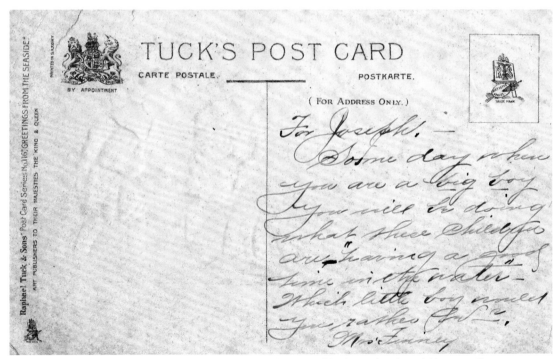

"For Joseph [Emma's baby son]—Some day when you are a big boy you will be doing what these children are—"having a good time in the water"—Which little boy would you rather be? Mrs. Finney"

An unmailed card, circa 1913. Postcard publisher: Tuck's Post Card, Raphael Tuck & Sons, England, "Greetings from the Seaside," Series No. 116.

Grand Canyon National Park, Arizona; Looking North from Yavapai Point.

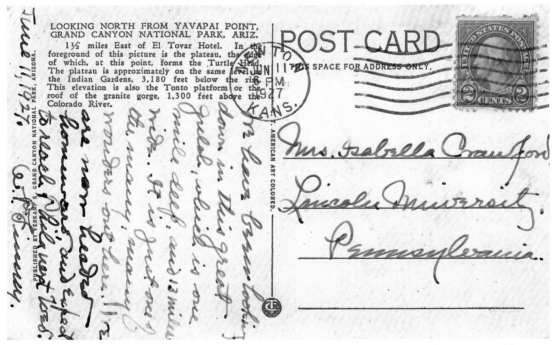

"June 11, 1927. We have been looking down in this great gulch, which is one mile deep, and 13 miles wide. It is just one of the many, many wonders out here. We are now headed homeward, and expect to reach Phila. Next Wed. W. P. Finney"

Mailed on June 11, 1927, to Isabella Crawford at home. Postcard publisher: Verkamp S., no. 78898.

Marie Lewis, Emma's Cousin, c. 1906.

been grateful that their generation had vastly greater access to education, that their family's fortunes were no longer tied to the land, and that, via their ties to Lincoln University, they were part of a larger world of Black Americans. They could have said of the preceding generations that they had borne the burden of racial prejudice successfully and were able, as Joseph Willson said in 1841, "to stand erect under their disabilities, and present a state of society of which . . . none have just cause to be ashamed."[93]

But for all the progress that their family and the mass of Black Americans had made during the nineteenth century, in the opening years of the new century they were harshly confronted with fundamental questions about their place in a country of hardening racial divisions. "The immediate future looks dark and troubled. I cannot shut my eyes to the ugly facts before me," Frederick Douglass observed bleakly in 1894, in his last major speech.[94]

And yet the Crawfords and their fellow African Americans pressed on, demonstrating a sense of agency inspired at its root by a characteristic mix of racial optimism and resilience that was captured by Mary Church Terrell in 1898:

And so, lifting as we climb, onward and upward we go, struggling and striving, and hoping that the buds and blossoms of our desires will burst into glorious fruition ere long. With courage, born of success achieved in the past, with a keen sense of the responsibility which we shall continue to assume, we look forward to a future large with promise and hope. Seeking no favors because of our color, nor patronage because of our needs, we knock at the bar of justice, asking an equal chance.[95]

Epilogue

This book covers the years of Emma Crawford's life from 1906 to 1910. She married a former Lincoln University student when she was twenty-three and never again worked outside the home—although she was far from idle. Soon she was busy with the first of what became a large Victorian family of twelve children. With the help of her mother, Isabella Crawford, Emma drilled multigenerational family values of respectability, achievement, and education into her children, with the result that theirs was the first Black family in Lincoln University village to graduate almost all of its offspring from high school (a son with a disability was the sole exception). Most Black villagers expected their children to enter domestic service, for which a high school education wasn't needed. However, from an early age, Emma and her husband's children were made aware that they would follow a different path. Ultimately, most of them attended college, which enabled them to take advantage of the widening scope of employment opportunities that the twentieth century offered for educated Black workers, although their options were still sharply limited by discriminatory laws and practices. They were worldly adults who settled in various East Coast cities, never losing an affection for their village upbringing.

All told, Emma and her husband did well for themselves and their family over the course of the twentieth century. But in the larger scheme of things, while these years were a period during which some conditions for Black Americans changed a great deal, progress was stymied by the fact that throughout the twentieth century, racial discrimination both persisted and took on new forms. "For every gain Black Americans made, people in power created new bundles of discrimination, largely hidden from sight, that thwarted, again and again, the economic promise of emancipation," writes historian Calvin Schermerhorn.[1] The bundles included restrictive covenants that limited where Black families could rent or buy houses, redlining that made Black households ineligible for federally guaranteed home loans, the exclusion of agricultural and domestic workers from Social Security, and a host of other policies and practices that resulted in deep racial inequities across social and economic sectors, including education, employment, political representation, health, and the justice system.[2] Reflecting the lack of racial economic progress over time, the typical white family now has eight times the wealth of the typical Black family, as reported by the Federal Reserve in 2020.[3]

One analysis of racial intergenerational mobility over the 120 years from 1880 to 2000 found that despite the changes in institutions, policies, and racial attitudes that have taken place over the past century, including the civil rights movement, Black children still do not enjoy the same economic outcomes as white children from households with similar economic characteristics.[4] Equally troubling, a large study that traced the lives of millions of children found that while white boys who grow up rich are likely to remain that way, even Black boys raised in high-income households are more likely to become poor than to stay wealthy as adults.[5] Such findings demonstrate that for structural reasons Black Americans experience significant challenges to moving out of poverty and sustaining intergenerational economic progress.

Today, the fact, and legacy, of structural racism is openly acknowledged and discussed as never before. That's a step forward. But the work of changing that deeply entrenched structure and reversing its effects still lies ahead—and calls for a major social transformation. To see disturbing parallels between Emma's day and ours, we need look no further than a 1909 NAACP statement decrying the disenfranchisement of the Black vote in Georgia and the Supreme Court's failure to "pass squarely upon this disfranchisement of millions."[6] And a central question of the same document—"How far has [America] gone in assuring to each and every citizen, irrespective of color, the equality of opportunity and equality before the law, which underlie our American institutions and are guaranteed by the Constitution?"—is sadly as relevant today as the day it was asked.

To end, as we began, with W. E. B. Du Bois, the unfortunate truth is that "the Nation has not yet found peace from its sins; the freedman has not yet found in freedom his promised land."[7]

Acknowledgments

The sense of family with which I was raised is a foundational part of my identity, and I am grateful for this opportunity to tell the story of my ancestors. As I dug into their history, I felt profound respect for their ability to survive despite encountering so many obstacles, decade after decade. I would not be who I am today without their perseverance and belief in themselves. The wider society may have told them that they were inconsequential, but they lived a different truth.

In addition, I thank Adrienne Childs, Barbara Boyle Torrey, A. Lynn Bolles, Sandra Jackson, Diane Skerrett, and family members who encouraged me from the beginning to develop my ideas about Emma Crawford's postcard collection. Many years of research and writing followed, during which I tussled with finding the balance between Emma's personal story and the larger history of her times.

Craig W. Gill, director at the University Press of Mississippi, and Jessica Harris saw promise in an early draft, providing vital encouragement as well as valuable advice about the subsequent development of the manuscript. Reviewers Matthew Griffis and Waldo Martin also played important roles, contributing both enthusiasm for the manuscript and insights that strengthened it. Lisa Williams's thoughtful editing, along with the care and attention of the staff of the University Press of Mississippi, brought everything together.

My husband, Archie Brown, and daughter, Lex, have been constant sources of support since I began this project, and I thank them for that and for their patience over the years.

Notes

Introduction

1. J. Baldwin (1963), *The Fire Next Time* (New York: Dial Press), pp. 116–17.
2. Matthew Griffis, personal communication, January 23, 2020.
3. W.E. B. Du Bois (1900), The American Negro at Paris, *The American Monthly Review of Reviews* 22(5) (London: Horace Marshall & Son), pp.575–77, Retrieved June 27, 2021, http://www.webdubois.org/dbANParis.html.

Chapter One: What Stories Can Postcards Tell?

1. R. Ellison (2011), *The Collected Essays of Ralph Ellison* (New York: Modern Library), p. 751, https://www.google.com/books/edition/The_Collected_Essays_of_Ralph_Ellison/GT3oSgZKvQoC?hl=en&gbpv=1&dq=the+collected+essays+of+ralph+ellison&printsec=frontcover.
2. L. Litwack (1998), *Trouble in Mind: Black Southerners in the Age of Jim Crow* (New York: Alfred E. Knopf), p. xvi.
3. F. Bassett (n.d.), *Wish You Were Here! The Story of the Golden Age of Picture Postcards in the United States* (New York State Library, Manuscripts and Special Collections), Retrieved April 18, 2020, from http://www.nysl.nysed.gov/msscfa/qc16510ess.htm.
4. D. B. Ryan (1982), *Picture Postcards in the United States, 1893–1918* (New York: Potter), pp. 22, 28.
5. Bassett, *Wish You Were Here!*
6. E. Strain (2003), *Public Places, Private Journeys: Ethnography, Entertainment, and the Tourist Gaze* (New Brunswick: Rutgers University Press), p. 39.
7. Bassett, *Wish You Were Here!*
8. Ryan, *Picture Postcards in the United States*, p. 28.
9. Library of Congress (n.d.), *Rise of Industrial America, 1876–1900*, Retrieved April 18, 2020, from http://www.loc.gov/teachers/classroommaterials/presentationsandactivities/presentations/timeline/riseind/.
10. The Coon Caricature (n.d.), Jim Crow Museum of Racist Memorabilia (Ferris State University), Retrieved July 2, 2021, from https://www.ferris.edu/jimcrow/coon/.
11. W. E. B. Du Bois (1911), Editorial, Colored Men Lynched without Trial, *The Crisis* 1(3) (New York: National Association for the Advancement of Colored People), p. 26, retrieved from https://modjourn.org/issue/bdr507847/.
12. A. Lee (2007), Introduction, in D. Apel & S. Smith, *Lynching Photographs* (Berkeley: University of California Press), p. 4.
13. D. Apel (2007), Lynching Photographs and Public Shaming, in D. Apel & S. Smith, *Lynching Photographs* (Berkeley: University of California Press), pp. 42–78.

14. M. Simpson (2004), Archiving Hate: Lynching Postcards at the Limit of Social Circulation. *ESC: English Studies in Canada 30*(1), pp. 17–38, retrieved July 2, 2021, from https://muse.jhu.edu/article/689499/pdf.

15. C. Lewis (1908), Race Progress! Louisville and Her Host of Thriving Afro-American Citizens (1908), *The Indianapolis Freeman*, p. 2, retrieved July 2, 2021, from https://news.google.com/newspapers?nid=FIkAGs9z2eEC&dat=19081226&printsec=frontpage&hl=en.

16. S. Otfinoski (2003), *African Americans in the Visual Arts* (New York: Facts on File, Inc.), pp. 17–18, retrieved July 2, 2021, from https://www.google.com/books/edition/African_Americans_in_the_Visual_Arts/BcWHdpRoDkUC?hl=en&gbpv=1&bsq=battey.

Chapter Two: The Status of the Negro in This Country

1. NationMaster (n.d.), *Economy > GDP per Capita in 1900: Countries Compared*, retrieved April 18, 2020, from https://www.nationmaster.com/country-info/stats/Economy/GDP-per-capita-in-1900.

2. R. Logan (1954), *The Negro in American Life and Thought: The Nadir, 1877–1901* (New York: Dial Press).

3. R. McGill (1965), *The Atlantic Online: W. E. B. DuBois*, https://www.theatlantic.com/past/docs/unbound/flashbks/black/mcgillbh.htm.

4. Editorial (1911), *The Crisis, 2*(2), p. 63, Retrieved June 28, 2021, from Modernist Journals Project, modjourn.org/issue/bdr522172/.

5. History.com (2021), *NAACP*, retrieved May 18, 2021, from https://www.history.com/topics/civil-rights-movement/naacp.

6. W. E. B. Du Bois (1903), *The Souls of Black Folk* (New York: Dover), p. 9, retrieved April 18, 2020, from https://www.gutenberg.org/files/408/408-h/408-h.htm.

7. D. Ham (1993), *The African-American Mosaic: A Library of Congress Resource Guide for the Study of Black History and Culture* (Washington, DC: Library of Congress), p. 118.

8. F. Hobbs & N. Stoops, N. (2002). *Demographic Trends in the 20th Century*. Washington, DC: US Census Bureau.

9. US Census Bureau (1980), *The Social and Economic Status of the Black Population in the United States: An Historical View, 1790–1978*, Special Studies, P-Series, Report No. 23–80 (Washington, DC: US Census Bureau, Current Population Reports).

10. P. Bergman (1969), *The Chronological History of the Negro in America* (New York: Harper & Row), p. 327.

11. T. Maloney (2002), *African Americans in the Twentieth Century*, Economic History Association, retrieved April 18, 2020, from https://eh.net/encyclopedia/african-americans-in-the-twentieth-century/.

12. L. Osborne (2003). Introduction, in T. L. Congress, *A Small Nation of People: W.E.B. Du Bois & African American Portraits of Progress* (New York: Amistad), p. 13.

13. M. Harris (1899). *Negro Womanhood*, Public Opinion, retrieved April 18, 2020, from https://www.google.com/books/edition/Public_Opinion/SIY-AQAAMAAJ?hl=en&gbpv=1&dq=Negro+womanhood.+Mrs.+L.+H.+Harris.&pg=PA812&printsec=frontcover.

14. *The Colored American Magazine* (1900), Editorial and Publisher's Announcements, p. 61, retrieved August 10, 2020, from https://babel.hathitrust.org/cgi/pt?id=uc1.b3793660&view=2up&seq=72&q1=the%20south%20is%20attempting.

15. E. Foner (2020), *Reconstruction*, retrieved April 18, 2020, from https://www.britannica.com/event/Reconstruction-United-States-history.

16. Facing History and Ourselves (n.d.), *The Reconstruction Acts of 1867*, retrieved April 18, 2020, from https://www.facinghistory.org/reconstruction-era/reconstruction-acts-1867.

17. R. Gibson (n.d.), *Booker T. Washington and W. E. B. Du Bois: The Problem of Negro Leadership*, retrieved April 18, 2020, from https://teachersinstitute.yale.edu/curriculum/units/1978/2/78.02.02.x.html.

18. Foner, *Reconstruction*.

19. Library of Congress (n.d.), *African American Timeline: 1850 to 1925*, retrieved April 18, 2020, from https://www.loc.gov/collections/african-american-perspectives-rare-books/articles-and-essays/timeline-of-african-american-history/1901-to-1925/.

20. T. Riis (1989), *Just Before Jazz; Black Musical Theater in New York, 1890–1915* (Washington, DC: Smithsonian Institution), p. 164.

21. Race Feeling Grows Intense (1906, April 17), *Augusta Chronicle*, Augusta, Georgia, retrieved August 10, 2020, from https://augustachronicle.newsbank.com/search?text=race%20feeling%20grows%20intense&content_added=&date_from=&date_to=&pub%5B0%5D=1252FEAF2D2D3A44.

22. K. Janken (2001), Introduction, in W. White, *Rope and Faggot; A Biography of Judge Lynch* (Notre Dame: University of Notre Dame Press), p. xiii.

23. The Atlanta Massacre (1906), *The Indianapolis Freeman*, p. 4, retrieved April 18, 2020, from http://news.google.com/newspapers?nid=FIkAGs9z2eEC&dat=19060929&printsec=frontpage&hl=en.

24. R. Wormser (n.d.), *The Rise and Fall of Jim Crow*, retrieved February 10, 2022, from https://www.thirteen.org/wnet/jimcrow/index.html.

25. Bergman, *Chronological History*, p. 348.

26. J. Crouthamel (1960), The Springfield Race Riot of 1908, *Journal of Negro History* 45, retrieved April 18, 2020, from pp. 65–81, http://www.jstor.org/stable/2716259.

27. C. Merritt (2008), *Something So Horrible: The Springfield Race Riot of 1908*, retrieved April 18, 2020, from https://www.illinois.gov/alplm/museum/Education/Documents/Race_Riot_Catalog_2008.pdf.

28. Bergman, *Chronological History*, p. 352.

29. NAACP (2008), *NAACP Leaders Mark 100th Anniversary of Springfield Race Riot*, https://www.naacp.org/latest/naacp-leaders-mark-100th-anniversary-of-springfield-race-riot/.

30. B. T. Washington (1908), Wants Justice for Negro: Booker T. Washington Makes Another Plea, *The Indianapolis Freeman*, p. 1, retrieved April 18, 2020, from https://news.google.com/newspapers?nid=FIkAGs9z2eEC&dat=19080829&printsec=frontpage&hl=en.

31. A. B. Wang & F. Sonmez (2022), Biden Signs Bill Making Lynching a Federal Hate Crime, *The Washington Post*, https://www.washingtonpost.com/politics/2022/03/29/biden-signs-bill-lynching-hate-crime/.

32. US Census Bureau, *Social and Economic Status of the Black Population*.

33. Bergman, *Chronological History*, p. 329.

34. W. E. B. Du Bois (1900), *The College-Bred Negro: Report of a Social Study Made under the Direction of Atlanta University* (Atlanta: Atlanta University Press), retrieved July 18, 2020, from https://www.google.com/books/edition/The_College_bred_Negro/qm42AAAAMAAJ?hl=en&gbpv=0.

35. Gibson, *Booker T. Washington and W. E. B. Du Bois*.

36. B. T. Washington (1896, September), The Awakening of the Negro, *The Atlantic*, retrieved September 20, 2020, from https://www.theatlantic.com/magazine/archive/1896/09/the-awakening-of-the-negro/305449/.

37. George Mason University (n.d.), *Booker T. Washington Delivers the 1895 Atlanta Compromise Speech*, retrieved April 18, 2020, from http://historymatters.gmu.edu/d/39/.

38. Gibson, *Booker T. Washington and W. E. B. Du Bois*.

39. Gibson, *Booker T. Washington and W. E. B. Du Bois*.

40. W. E. B. Du Bois, *The Souls of Black Folk*, p. 31.

41. W. E. B. Du Bois, *The Souls of Black Folk*, pp. 55–67.

42. R. Ater (2011), *Remaking Race and History: The Sculpture of Meta Warrick Fuller* (Berkeley: University of California Press), p. 39.

43. *Not Pity but Respect* (1906), *Alexander's Magazine*, pp. 18–19, https://hdl.handle.net/2027/inu.30000117863757?urlappend=%3Bseq=27.

44. M. Russo (2005), *Hinsonville, a Community at the Crossroads: The Story of a Nineteenth-Century African-American Village* (Selinsgrove, PA: Susquehanna University Press), p. 65.

45. Harris, *Negro Womanhood*.

46. W. E. B. Du Bois (1898), *Some Efforts of American Negroes for Their Own Social Betterment. Report of an Investigation under the Direction of Atlanta University; Together with the Proceedings of the Third Conference for the Study of the Negro Problems, Held at Atlanta University*, retrieved April 18, 2020, from https://docsouth.unc.edu/church/duboisau/dubois.html

47. D. Bruce (1989), *Black American Writing from the Nadir: The Evolution of a Literary Tradition, 1877–1915* (Baton Rouge: Louisiana State University Press), pp. 1–10.

48. US Census Bureau, *Social and Economic Status of the Black Population*.

49. Litwack, *Trouble in Mind*, p. 160.

50. Litwack, *Trouble in Mind*, p. 160.

51. W. E. B. Du Bois (1934), *A Negro Nation within a Nation*, retrieved April 18, 2020, from https://www.blackpast.org/african-american-history/1934-w-e-b-du-bois-negro-nation-within-nation/.

52. L. Baldwin (1983), *"Invisible" Strands in African Methodism: A History of the African Union Methodist Protestant and Union American Methodist Episcopal Churches, 1805–1980* (Metuchen, NJ: American Theological Library Association, and London: Scarecrow Press).

53. M. Work (1913), *Fifty Years of Negro Progress* 6(10), (Washington, DC: Associated Publishers, Inc.), Retrieved June 11, 2021, from https://hdl.handle.net/2027/emu.10002331968?urlappend=%3Bseq=7.

54. Office for Civil Rights, US Dept. of Education (1991), *Historically Black Colleges and Universities and Higher Education Desegregation*, Retrieved April 18, 2020, from https://www2.ed.gov/about/offices/list/ocr/docs/hq9511.html.

55. G. Lerner (1974), Early Community Work of Black Club Women, *The Journal of Negro History, 59*(2), pp. 158–67, Retrieved July 25, 2020, from https://www.jstor.org/stable/2717327.

56. W. E. B. Du Bois, *Some Efforts of American Negroes for Their Own Social Betterment*.

57. D. Willis (2003), The Sociologist's Eye: W. E. B. Du Bois and the Paris Exposition, In T. L. Congress, *A Small Nation of People: W. E. B. Du Bois & African American Portraits of Progress* (New York: Amistad), p. 55.

Chapter Three: Fighting for Their Daily Bread

1. E. Clark-Lewis (1994), *Living In, Living Out: African American Domestics in Washington, D.C., 1910–1940* (Washington, DC: Smithsonian Institution Press), pp. 12–13.

2. H. Gannett (1895), *Occupations of the Negroes* (Baltimore: The Trustees), p. 6, Retrieved June 11, 2021, from https://hdl.handle.net/2027/nnc2.ark:/13960/t6qz65x3h?urlappend=%3Bseq=8.

3. W. E. B. Du Bois & A. Dill (1914), *Morals and Manners among Negro Americans* (Atlanta: Atlanta University Publications).

4. Du Bois & Dill, *Morals and Manners among Negro Americans*; spelling modernized by the author.

5. W. E. B. Du Bois (1899), *The Philadelphia Negro: A Social Study* (New York: Schocken Books), pp. 97–146.

6. M. Hurley (1997), *The Average Yearly Salaries of All Industries Excluding Farm Labor*, Retrieved April 20, 2020, from https://web.bryant.edu/~ehu/h364proj/sprg_97/hurley/salary.html.

7. Clark-Lewis, *Living In, Living Out*, pp. 131, 147.

8. Clark-Lewis, *Living In, Living Out*, p. 106.

9. C. Leon (2016). *The Life of American Workers in 1915*, Retrieved January 30, 2020, from https://www.bls.gov/opub/mlr/2016/article/the-life-of-american-workers-in-1915.htm.

10. I. Eaton (1899), Special Report on Negro Domestic Service in the Seventh Ward, Philadelphia, In W. E. B. Du Bois, *The Philadelphia Negro: A Social Study* (New York: Schocken), pp. 425–509.

11. Leon, *Life of American Workers in 1915*.

12. *Philadelphia Zoo Gatehouses* (n.d.), Retrieved April 8, 2018, from https://philly.curbed.com/maps/best-frank-furness-projects-philadelphia/philadelphia-zoo-gatehouses.

13. Clark-Lewis, *Living In, Living Out*, p. 99.

14. A. Hassan (2018), A Postcard View of African-American Life, *The New York Times*, https://www.nytimes.com/2018/02/24/us/a-postcard-view-of-african-american-life.html.

15. PBS (n.d.), *The African Americans: Many Rivers to Cross*, Retrieved April 20, 2020, from Racist Images and Messages in Jim Crow Era, https://www.pbs.org/video/african-americans-many-rivers-cross-racist-images-and-messages-jim-crow-era/.

16. Eaton, *Special Report*.

17. The Friends Meeting (1915), *Two Hundredth Anniversary of the Establishment of The Friends Meeting at New Garden Chester County, Pennsylvania*, Retrieved April 12, 2021, from https://www.ancestry.com/search/collections/10661/.

18. R. Tyson (n.d.), *Our First Friends, the Quakers*, Retrieved April 20, 2020, from Pennsylvania Heritage, http://www.phmc.state.pa.us/portal/communities/pa-heritage/our-first-friends-early-quakers.html.

19. Tyson, *Our First Friends*.

20. C. Densmore (n.d.), *Quakers and the Underground Railroad: Myths and Realities*, Retrieved April 20, 2020, from http://web.tricolib.brynmawr.edu/speccoll/quakersandslavery/commentary/organizations/underground_railroad.php.

21. J. Bodnar (1997), The Impact of the "New Immigration" on the Black Worker: Steelton, Pennsylvania, 1880–1920, In J. W. Trotter & E. L. Smith (Eds.), *African Americans in Pennsylvania: Shifting Historical Perspectives* (Harrisburg: The Pennsylvania

Historical and Museum Commission and University Park: Pennsylvania State University Press), pp. 257–71.

22. In 1948 Mercy merged with Douglass Hospital, founded in 1895 also to serve Philadelphia's Black community. The former Mercy-Douglass site is now the home of the Woodland Avenue Health Center.

23. Eaton, *Special Report.*

24. Philadelphia Area Archives Research Portal (n.d.), *Conard-Pyle Company Records*, Retrieved July 13, 2020, from http://dla.library.upenn.edu/dla/pacscl/ead .html?id=PACSCL_UDel_UDelMSS634.

25. *Boyd's Chester County, Pennsylvania Directory* (1896–97) (Philadelphia: C. E. Howe), p. 515, https://www.ancestry.com/search/collections/10689/.

26. C. Shane (2011, April 4), Why the Dearth of Statues Honoring Women in Statuary Hall and Elsewhere? *The Washington Post*, https://www.washingtonpost.com/life style/style/why-the-dearth-of-statues-honoring-women-in-statuary-hall-and-else where/2011/04/11/AFx8lgjD_story.html.

27. N. Fiorellini (2020, August 3), Statue of White Woman Holding Hatchet and Scalps Sparks Backlash in New England, *The Guardian*, https://www.theguardian.com/ us-news/2020/aug/03/hannah-duston-statue-new-hampshire-native-americans.

28. Wright Realtors (n.d.), *Stockton Midtown Houses*, Retrieved April 21, 2020, from https://www.wrightrealtors.com/stockton/houses-midtown.htm.

29. Historic Kennett Square (n.d.), *Kennett Square Walking Tour*, Retrieved February 15, 2020, from https://historickennettsquare.com/about/history/walking-tour/.

30. Eaton, *Special Report*, p. 481.

31. Eaton, *Special Report.*

32. Deserts Heir to Riches on Her Way to the Altar (1907), *The News-Democrat* (Providence, RI), p. 8, http://news.google.com/newspapers?id=TCBbAAAAIBAJ&s jid=oE4NAAAAIBAJ&pg=1076,4223046&dq=wilson-howe&hl=en.

33. Deserts Heir to Riches on Her Way to the Altar, p. 8.

34. Christmas Frolics at the White House from the Time of Washington to the Present Day (1913, December 12), *The Evening Star* (Washington, DC), p. 3, Retrieved April 21, 2020, from https://chroniclingamerica.loc.gov/lccn/sn83045462/1913-12-21/ed-1/seq-55/.

35. Wife of Woodrow Wilson's Nephew Found Dead (1928, April 12), *Border Cities Star*, p. 1, https://news.google.com/newspapers?id=ScFEAAAAIBAJ&sjid=Oro MAAAAIBAJ&pg=1693,3626684&dq=virgini.

36. R. Taylor, L. Chatters, A.Woodward, & E. Brown (2013). *Racial and Ethnic Differences in Extended Family, Friendship, Fictive Kin and Congregational Informal Support Networks*, US National Library of Medicine, https://www.ncbi.nlm.nih.gov/ pmc/articles/PMC4116141/.

37. A. Lafrance (2016, October), The Weird Familiarity of 100-Year-Old Feminism Memes, *The Atlantic*, Retrieved February 17, 2020, from https://www.theatlantic.com/ technology/archive/2016/10/pepe-the-anti-suffrage-frog/505406/.

38. Boston University (2015), *William Keylor in City Journal: Wilson's Racism*, Retrieved April 21, 2020, from https://www.bu.edu/pardeeschool/2015/10/08/ william-keylor-in-city-journalwilsons-racism/.

39. A. Meier (1963), *Negro Thought in America, 1880–1915: Racial Ideologies in the Age of Booker T. Washington* (Ann Arbor: University of Michigan Press), pp. 187–88.

40. J. Smith (2008), *FDR* (New York: Random House), p. 99.

41. W. E. B. Du Bois (1913), *Open Letter to Woodrow Wilson*, https://teachingameri canhistory.org/library/document/open-letter-to-woodrow-wilson/.

Chapter Four: Romance and Friendship

1. F. Foster (2008), *Love and Marriage in Early African America* (Boston: Northeastern University Press), p. 92.

2. Fifty-one percent of men and 43 percent of women over fifteen years old for the Black population, compared to 52 percent of men and 49 percent of women for whites.

3. Some 1.1 percent compared to 0.3 percent.

4. W. E. B. Du Bois, *Philadelphia Negro*, p. 68.

5. US Census Bureau, *Social and Economic Status of the Black Population*.

6. G. Edwards & W. Cobb (1901). *I'll Be with You When the Roses Bloom Again*, SecondHandSongs, https://secondhandsongs.com/work/130096/all.

7. L. Montgomery (1908), *Anne of Green Gables*, https://www.gutenberg.org/files/45/45-h/45-h.htm.

8. The Atlantic City Experience (2020), http://www.atlanticcityexperience.org/index.php?option=com_content&view=article&id=10:northside-atlantic-city-black-community&catid=7&Itemid=11.

9. N. Johnson (2010), *The Northside: African Americans and the Creation of Atlantic City* (Medford: Plexus), ebook location 686.

10. Johnson, *The Northside*.

11. MonopolyCity.com. (2008), *Early Hotels—From Atlantic City's Nostalgic Past*, https://www.monopolycity.com/ac_earlyhotels.html.

12. Lincoln University (1918), *Lincoln University College and Theological Seminary: Biographical Catalogue 1918* (Lancaster: The New Era Printing Company), p. 94, http://www.lincoln.edu/library/specialcollections/alumnimagazine/1918.pdf.

13. Strain, *Public Places, Private Journeys*, pp. 32–33.

14. Lincoln University (1909). *Lincoln University Herald* (Lincoln University, Pennsylvania) p. 9, https://www.lincoln.edu/sites/default/files/library/specialcollections/herald/1909.pdf.

15. Du Bois, *Philadelphia Negro*, p. 321.

16. Tuck DB Postcards (n.d.), *History of Raphael Tuck & Sons LTD*, https://tuckdbpostcards.org/history.

17. Ryan, *Picture Postcards in the United States*, p. 201.

18. Pennsylvania Historical & Museum Commission (2015), *Historic Agricultural Resources of Pennsylvania c 1700–1960*, Pennsylvania Agricultural History Project, http://www.phmc.state.pa.us/portal/communities/agriculture/history/index.html.

19. J. Kornacki (2015), General Strike of 1910, in *The Encyclopedia of Greater Philadelphia*, https://philadelphiaencyclopedia.org/archive/general-strike-of-1910/.

20. The Historical Marker Database (2019), *The John A. Wilson Building*, https://www.hmdb.org/m.asp?m=65712.

Chapter Five: On the Road with the Minstrel Show

1. Riis, *Just before Jazz*, p. 4.

2. R. Barnes (2016), *Darkology: The Hidden History of Amateur Blackface Minstrelsy and the Making of Modern America, 1860–1970*, Retrieved May 18, 2021, from Harvard Library, Office for Scholarly Communication, https://dash.harvard.edu/handle/1/33493592.

3. J. Sturcke (2009, Feb. 5), Golliwog Began as Beloved Children's Character, *The Guardian*, https://www.theguardian.com/world/2009/feb/05/golliwog-history-flor ence-kate-upton.

4. R. Toll (1974), *Blacking Up: The Minstrel Show in 19th-Century America* (London: Oxford University Press), p. 223.

5. Toll, *Blacking Up*, p. 223.

6. G. Sorin (2020), *Driving While Black: African American Travel and the Road to Civil Rights* (New York: Liveright), p. x.

7. S. Wendell (1990), Oppression and Victimization; Choice and Responsibility, *Hypatia* 5(3), pp. 15-46, Retrieved July 10, 2021, from https://www.jstor.org/stable/3809974.

8. P. Dunbar (1895), *We Wear the Mask*, poetryfoundation.org/poems/44203/ we-wear-the-mask.

9. Digital Public Library of America (1922), *A Draft Eulogy Written by W. E. B. Du Bois about Bert Williams*, Retrieved May 22, 2021, from https://dp.la/primary -source-sets/blackface-minstrelsy-in-modern-america/sources/1436.

10. *Jim Crow: A Comic Song Sung by Mr. Rice at the Chestnut St. Theatre* (1832), Philadelphia: J. Edgar. Edison Collection of American Sheet Music. https://hdl.handle .net/2027/mdp.39015096384907?urlappend=%3Bseq=2%3Bownerid=114188231-1.

11. Toll, *Blacking Up*, p. 30.

12. E. Southern (1997), *The Music of Black Americans, Third Edition* (New York: W. W. Norton), p. 43.

13. L. Emery (1988), *Black Dance from 1619 to Today, Second Edition* (Trenton, NJ: Princeton Book Company), p. 185.

14. Southern, *Music of Black Americans*, p. 95.

15. C. Dickens (1913), *American Notes for General Circulation*, Retrieved April 29, 2020, from Project Gutenberg, https://www.gutenberg.org/files/675/675-h/675-h.htm.

16. Toll, *Blacking Up*, p. 50.

17. Toll, *Blacking Up*, p. 66.

18. *Jim Crow Museum of Racist Memorabilia* (n.d.), Ferris State University, Retrieved May 12, 2020, from https://ferris.edu/jimcrow/.

19. S. Foster (1848), *Old Uncle Ned*, Song of America, https://songofamerica.net/ song/old-uncle-ned/.

20. E. Southern (1996), The Georgia Minstrels: The Early Years, In A. J. Bean, *Inside the Minstrel Mask: Readings in 19th-Century Blackface Minstrelsy* (Hanover, NH: Wesleyan University Press), p. 164.

21. Southern, *Music of Black Americans*, p. 232.

22. H. Sampson (1988), *The Ghost Walks: A Chronological History of Blacks in Show Business, 1865–1910* (London: Scarecrow Press), p. 283.

23. Toll, *Blacking Up*, p. 211.

24. Colorado Encyclopedia (n.d.), *Tabor Grand Opera House*, Retrieved May 12, 2020, from https://coloradoencyclopedia.org/article/tabor-grand-opera-house.

25. Riis, *Just before Jazz*, p. 4.

26. Southern, *Music of Black Americans*, p. 236.

27. L. Abbott & D. Seroff (2002), *Out of Sight: The Rise of African American Popular Music, 1889–1895* (Jackson: University Press of Mississippi), p. 65.

28. Riis, *Just before Jazz*, p. 4.

29. Ham, *African-American Mosaic*, p. 150.

30. History of Minstrelsy (n.d.), *Ragtime and the "Coon Song,"* Retrieved May 12, 2020, from http://exhibits.lib.usf.edu/exhibits/show/minstrelsy/jimcrow-to-jolson/ ragtime-and-the-coon-song.

31. L. Hudson (2008), "Entertaining Citizenship: Masculinity and Minstrelsy in Post-Emancipation San Francisco," *The Journal of African American History*, 93(2), pp. 174–97, http://www.jstor.org/stable/25609967.

32. Riis, *Just before Jazz*, p. 100.

33. R. Lewis (2007), *From Traveling Show to Vaudeville: Theatrical Spectacle in America, 1830–1910* (Baltimore: Johns Hopkins University Press), https://www.google.com/books/edition/From_Traveling_Show_to_Vaudeville/ijl-W-QoacMC?hl=en&gbpv=1&dq=From%20Traveling%20Show%20to%20Vaudeville%3A%20Theatrical%20Spectacle%20in%20America%2C%201830-1910&pg=PA1&printsec=frontcover&bsq=From%20Traveling%20Show%.

34. Sampson, *Ghost Walks*, p. 283.

35. W. Lewis (2003), *A Brief History of African American Marching Bands*, Retrieved May 12, 2020, from Folkstreams, http://www.folkstreams.net/film-context.php?id=249.

36. Lewis, *Brief History of African American Marching Bands*.

37. L. Abbott & D. Seroff, *Ragged but Right: Black Traveling Shows, "Coon Songs," and the Dark Pathway to Blues and Jazz* (Jackson: University Press of Mississippi), ebook loc. 4243.

38. Toll, *Blacking Up*, p. 225.

39. Toll, *Blacking Up*, p. 228.

40. E. Isaacs (1947), *The Negro in the American Theatre* (New York: Theatre Arts), p. 31.

41. Abbott & Seroff, *Out of Sight*, p. xi.

42. Toll, *Blacking Up*, p. 219.

43. Sorin, *Driving While Black*, p. x.

44. Abbott & Seroff, *Ragged but Right*, loc. 2225.

45. Notes from Al. E. Holman's Band and Serenaders, Now Touring Europe with the J. T. McCaddon's Company (1905), *The Indianapolis Freeman*, p. 5, https://news.google.com/newspapers?nid=FIkAGs9z2eEC&dat=19050506&printsec=frontpage&hl=en.

46. J. T. McCaddon Arrested: American Whose Circus Failed Accused of Fraudulent Bankruptcy (1905), *The New York Times*, p. 2, https://timesmachine.nytimes.com/timesmachine/1905/10/01/101331270.html?pageNumber=2.

47. Princeton University (n.d.), *McCaddon Collection of the Barnum and Bailey Circus 1871–1907*, Retrieved May 15, 2020, from Princeton University Library Manuscripts Division, http://arks.princeton.edu/ark:/88435/02870v897.

48. Abbott & Seroff, *Out of Sight*, p. 106.

49. Toll, *Blacking Up*, p. 228.

50. Abbott & Seroff, *Out of Sight*, p. 106.

51. Abbott & Seroff, *Out of Sight*, p. 107.

52. Sampson, *Ghost Walks*, p. 258.

53. L. Levine (1977), *Black Culture and Black Consciousness* (New York: Oxford University Press), pp. 298–366.

54. Old Comedian Dead (1915, July 1), *Artesia Pecos Valley News*, https://newspaperarchive.com/other-articles-clipping-jul-01-1915-229432/.

55. Abbott & Seroff, *Ragged but Right*, ebook loc. 210.

56. J. Davis (2014), Variety Shows, Minstrelsy, and Social Aesthetics during the Virginia Encampment of 1863–64, *The Virginia Magazine of History and Biography*, 122(2), pp. 128–55, Retrieved May 28, 2021, from http://www.jstor.org/stable/24393923.

57. *The Coconino Sun* (1906, February 10), Retrieved August 10, 2020, from untitled article, https://chroniclingamerica.loc.gov/lccn/sn87062055/1906-02-10/ed-1/seq-3/.

58. M. Hearn (2013), *Saucy Postcards: The Bamforth Collection* (United Kingdom: Little, Brown Book Group Limited), https://www.google.com/books/edition/Saucy_Postcards_The_Bamforth_Collection/bq2aDwAAQBAJ?hl=en&gbpv=0.

59. P. Watt (2017), *Cheap Print and Popular Song in the Nineteenth Century* (Cambridge: Cambridge University Press), Retrieved May 22, 2020, from https://books.google.com/books?id=V3U3DgAAQBAJ&dq=song+i%27se+a+waiting+for+you+josie&source=gbs_navlinks_s.

60. I's A-Waiting for You, Josie (n.d.), Retrieved May 22, 2020, from https://monologues.co.uk/musichall/Songs-I/Is-Awaiting-For-You-Josie.htm.

61. N. Ward (2016), *A Brief History of the Pantomime—And Why It's About So Much More Than 'Blokes in Dresses,'* Retrieved February 26, 2022, from https://theconversation.com/a-brief-history-of-the-pantomime-and-why-its-about-so-much-more-than-blokes-in-dresses-69683.

62. P. Morton (1991), *Disfigured Images: The Historical Assault on Afro-American Women* (New York: Praeger), pp. 1–15.

63. D. Brooks & L. Hébert (2006), Gender, Race, and Media Representation, In B. Dow & J. Wood, *The SAGE Handbook of Gender and Communication* (Thousand Oaks, CA: SAGE), pp. 297–318, Retrieved May 28, 2021, from https://us.corwin.com/sites/default/files/upm-binaries/11715_Chapter16.pdf.

64. University of Saskatchewan (n.d.), *Ambisextrous: Gender Impersonators of Music Hall and Vaudeville*, Retrieved May 28, 2021, from http://digital.scaa.sk.ca/gallery/genderimpersonators/.

65. A. Semuels (2016), The Racist History of Portland, the Whitest City in America, *The Atlantic*, https://www.theatlantic.com/business/archive/2016/07/racist-history-portland/492035/.

66. The Georgia Minstrels (1906), *Daily Capital Journal*, p. 6, Retrieved May 22, 2020, from Library of Congress, Chronicling America, https://chroniclingamerica.loc.gov/lccn/sn99063957/1906-09-27/ed-1/seq-6.

67. K. Clark (2008), *Shasta Springs—Forgotten Resort*, Retrieved July 13, 2020, from http://shastasprings.com/Resort/.

68. Sampson, *Ghost Walks*, pp. 391–92.

69. South Carolina (1907, April 27), *New York Dramatic Mirror*, p. 8.

70. The History of Esko and Thomson Township (2016), Retrieved May 22, 2020, from http://www.eskohistory.com/gallery/image/762211/3383851.

71. City of Tumwater, Washington (2020), *About Tumwater: History*, Retrieved July 13, 2020, from https://www.ci.tumwater.wa.us/about-tumwater/history#:~:text=When%20the%20City%20was%20founded,other%20points%20on%20Puget%20Sound.

72. R. Hatanaka (2019), *Streetcars before Buses: British Columbia Electric Railway*, Retrieved May 26, 2020, from https://digitize.library.ubc.ca/digitizers-blog/streetcars-before-buses-british-columbia-electric-railway/.

73. The Bancroft Library (2006), *The 1906 San Francisco Earthquake and Fire*, Retrieved May 26, 2020, from https://bancroft.berkeley.edu/collections/earthquakeandfire/exhibit/room03.html.

74. Sampson, *Ghost Walks*, pp. 416–17.

75. Santa Monica History Museum (2020), *Santa Monica History*, Retrieved July 13, 2020, from https://santamonicahistory.org/santa-monica-history/.

76. T. Tzeng (2011), Eastern Promises: The Role of Eastern Capital in the Development of Los Angeles, 1900–1920, *California History* 88(2), p. 32, https://doi.org/10.2307/23052268.

77. City of San Bernardino California (n.d.), *About San Bernardino*, Retrieved May 26, 2020, from http://www.sbcity.org/about/default.asp.

78. T. Palmer (1897), *The Jack Rabbits of the United States* (Washington, DC: Government Printing Office), https://books.google.com/books?id=t9ArAAAAYAAJ&ppis=_e&printsec=frontcover&source=gbs_ge_summary_r&cad=0#v=onepage&q&f=false.

79. Illinois Health News (1912), *Illinois Health News; Volume 8*, https://www.google.com/books/edition/Illinois_Health_News/4wIgAQAAMAAJ?hl=en&gbpv=0.

80. A. Anderson (2000), *Snake Oil, Hustlers and Hambones: The American Medicine Show* (Jefferson, NC: McFarland), p. 101, https://www.google.com/books/edition/Snake_Oil_Hustlers_and_Hambones/FRSBCgAAQBAJ?hl=en&gbpv=1&dq=Ann+Anderson+Snake+Oil,+Hustlers+and+Hambones&printsec=frontcover.

81. Comstock House (2013), *On Tuesday the Monster Came to Town*, Retrieved May 26, 2020, from http://comstockhousehistory.blogspot.com/2013/02/on-tuesday-monster-came-to-town.html.

82. The Great Ferdon Co. No. 2 (1908), *The Indianapolis Freeman*, page 5, Retrieved July 21, 2020, from https://news.google.com/newspapers?nid=FIkAGs9z2eEC&dat=19080919&printsec=frontpage&hl=en

83. Richards & Pringle's Minstrels: Holland & Filkings, Mgrs. (1909), *The Indianapolis Freeman*, p. 5, Retrieved July 21, 2020, from https://news.google.com/newspapers?nid=FIkAGs9z2eEC&dat=19090731&printsec=frontpage&hl=en.

84. S. Russell (1909), Opening of the Georgia Minstrels, *The Indianapolis Freeman*, p. 6, Retrieved May 26, 2020, from https://news.google.com/newspapers?nid=FIkAGs9z2eEC&dat=19090807&printsec=frontpage&hl=en.

85. Abbott & Seroff, *Ragged but Right*, ebook loc. 122.

86. Russell, Opening of the Georgia Minstrels, p. 6.

87. B. Little (2019), *How the Galveston Hurricane of 1900 Became the Deadliest U.S. Natural Disaster*, Retrieved May 26, 2020, from https://www.history.com/news/how-the-galveston-hurricane-of-1900-became-the-deadliest-u-s-natural-disaster.

88. Wichita Falls Texas (n.d.), *A Very Short History of Wichita Falls*, Retrieved May 26, 2020, from https://tx-wichitafalls3.civicplus.com/DocumentCenter/View/19746/Very-Short-History-of-WF?bidId=.

89. Negroes Were Mobbed (1909, November 2), *Palestine, Texas, Daily Herald*, Retrieved May 15, 2020, from https://chroniclingamerica.loc.gov/lccn/sn86090383/1909-11-02/ed-1/seq-1/.

90. Negro Slays Officer: Citizens Meet and Order Many Blacks to Leave Town (1907, April 27), *Bryan Morning Eagle*, Retrieved June 17, 2021, from https://chroniclingamerica.loc.gov/lccn/sn86088652/1907-04-27/ed-1/seq-2.

91. Fort Worth Telegram (1907), *The Waxahachie Daily Light*, p. 2, Retrieved June 17, 2021, from https://chroniclingamerica.loc.gov/lccn/sn86090369/1907-05-02/ed-1/seq-2/.

92. E. Jaspin (2018), Leave or Die: America's Hidden History of Racial Expulsions, *Austin-American Statesman*, https://www.statesman.com/news/20161014/leave-or-die-americas-hidden-history-of-racial-expulsions.

93. C. Yeomans (2018), Piece of History Lost after Jones Bridge Collapses into Chattahoochee River, *Gwinnett Daily Post*, https://www.gwinnettdailypost.com/local/piece-of-history-lost-after-jones-bridge-collapses-into-chattahoochee/article_1354b1b8-24c8-59fe-8bed-f3712d88b091.html.

94. Route (Richards & Pringle's Minstrels) (1910), *The Indianapolis Freeman*, p. 5, Retrieved June 11, 2021, from https://news.google.com/newspapers?nid=FIkAGs9z2eEC&dat=19100402&printsec=frontpage&hl=en.

95. Notable Kentucky African Americans (2018), *African American Schools in Christian County, Kentucky*, Retrieved May 26, 2020, from http://nkaa.uky.edu/nkaa/items/show/2649.

96. K. Leetaru (2011), *Mechanical Engineering Shop Laboratory/Wood Shop and Foundry Laboratory*, Retrieved May 26, 2020, from http://uihistories.library.illinois.edu/cgi-bin/cview?SITEID=1&ID=280.

97. W. Hewitt (1991), Wicked Traffic in Girls: Prostitution and Reform in Sioux City, 1885–1910, *The Annals of Iowa, 51*(2), pp. 123–48, doi: https://doi.org/10.17077/0003-4827.9577.

98. St. Cloud State University (n.d.), *History and Traditions*, Retrieved May 26, 2020, from https://www.stcloudstate.edu/studenthandbook/history-traditions.aspx.

99. Toll, *Blacking Up*, p. 273.

100. Sampson, *Ghost Walks*, p. 357.

101. Sampson, *Ghost Walks*, pp. 357–58.

Chapter Six: Struggling and Striving

1. F. Douglass (1848), *Address at the Celebration of West India Emancipation, Rochester, N.Y.*, Library of Congress, Retrieved May 29, 2020, from https://www.loc.gov/resource/mfd.21023/?sp=4&st=single.

2. Clark-Lewis, *Living In, Living Out*, p. 19.

3. N. Ellis (2020, February 25), Descendants, *The Washington Post*, https://www.washingtonpost.com/nation/2020/02/25/lost-lineage-quest-identify-black-americans-roots/?arc404=true.

4. Southern, *Music of Black Americans*, p. 103.

5. Africa! The Colored Population of Philadelphia (1867), *The Evening Telegraph*, p. 1, Retrieved July 13, 2020, from https://chroniclingamerica.loc.gov/lccn/sn83025925/1867-03-30/ed-1/seq-1/.

6. Pennsylvania Society for Promoting the Abolition of Slavery (1838), *The Present State and Condition of the Free People of Color, of the City of Philadelphia*, pp. 1–52, Retrieved May 29, 2020, from https://archive.org/details/presentstatecondoopenn.

7. L. Hopkins (2000), *Among These Hills: African Americans in Lancaster County's Southern End*, presentation to the Southern Lancaster County Historical Society.

8. Attitude of White Press (1908), *The Indianapolis Freeman*, p. 6, Retrieved June 18, 2021, from https://news.google.com/newspapers?nid=FIkAGs9z2eEC&dat=19080404&printsec=frontpage&hl=en.

9. D. Harper (2003), *Slavery in Pennsylvania*, http://slavenorth.com/pennsylvania.htm.

10. E. Turner (1969), *The Negro in Pennsylvania: Slavery—Servitude—Freedom, 1639–1861* (New York: Negro Universities Press), pp. 1–16.

11. G. Nash (1991), *Freedom by Degrees: Emancipation in Pennsylvania and Its Aftermath* (New York: Oxford University Press), p. 33.

12. T. Bouton (n.d.), *Slave, Free Black, and White Population, 1780–1830*, Retrieved May 31, 2020, from https://userpages.umbc.edu/~bouton/History407/SlaveStats.htm.

13. Nash, *Freedom by Degrees*, p. 37.

14. J. Soderlund (1983), Black Women in Colonial Pennsylvania, *The Pennsylvania Magazine of History and Biography 107*(1), p. 60, Retrieved July 12, 2021, from https://www.jstor.org/stable/20091739.

15. F. Ellis & S. Evans (1883), *History of Lancaster County, Pennsylvania: With Biographical Sketches of Many of Its Pioneers and Prominent Men* (Philadelphia: Everts & Peck), p. 690, https://www.google.com/books/edition/History_of_Lancaster_County_Pennsylvania/yX7IhoEQUaQC?hl=en&gbpv=0.

16. Hopkins, *Among These Hills.*

17. E. Smith (1998), The End of Black Voting Rights in Pennsylvania: African Americans and the Pennsylvania Consitutional Convention of 1837–1838, *Pennsylvania History* 65(3), p. 279, Retrieved May 31, 2020, from https://www.jstor.org/stable/27774118.

18. Nash, *Freedom by Degrees*, p. 193.

19. Hopkins, *Among These Hills.*

20. J. Jones (1999), *Remarks on Racial and Cultural Conflict in Chester County for the Discussion of the 1845 Edition of the Narrative of the Life of Frederick Douglass, an American Slave*, Retrieved May 31, 2020, from https://digitalcommons.wcupa.edu/cgi/viewcontent.cgi?article=1053&context=hist_wchest.

21. D. Harper (2003), *Race Relations in Pennsylvania*, Retrieved May 31, 2020, from http://slavenorth.com/pennrace.htm.

22. S. Harley (1978), Northern Black Female Workers: Jacksonian Era, In S. Harley, & R. Terborg-Penn (Eds.), *The Afro-American Woman*, pp. 5–16 (Port Washington, NY: Kennikat Press).

23. M. Malloy (1990), *African Americans in the Maritime Trades: A Guide to Resources in New England* (Sharon, MA: The Kendall Whaling Museum), Retrieved July 12, 2021, from https://www.whalingmuseum.org/sites/default/files/pdf/KWM%20Monograph%20Series%20No%206_African%20Americans.pdf.

24. New Bedford Whaling Museum (2018), *African-Americans in New Bedford*, Retrieved May 31, 2020, from https://www.whalingmuseum.org/learn/research-topics/cultural-communities#African-Americans%20in%20NB.

25. T. Juravich, W. Hartford, & J. Green (1996), *Commonwealth of Toil: Chapters in the History of Massachusetts Workers and Their Unions* (Amherst: University of Massachusetts Press), 34–35.

26. W. Bolster (1997), *Black Jacks: African American Seamen in the Age of Sail* (Cambridge: Harvard University Press), pp. 160–61.

27. K. DeVan (2008), *Our Most Famous Border: The Mason-Dixon Line*, Retrieved July 13, 2020, from https://www.pabook.libraries.psu.edu/literary-cultural-heritage-map-pa/feature-articles/our-most-famous-border-mason-dixon-line.

28. Hopkins, *Among These Hills.*

29. African Methodist Episcopal Church (n.d.), *Our History*, Retrieved June 18, 2021, from https://www.ame-church.com/our-church/our-history/.

30. Lititz Public Library (n.d.), *Historical African American Churches in Lancaster County*, Retrieved May 31, 2020, from https://lititzlibrary.org/historical-african-american-churches-in-lancaster-county/.

31. Southern Lancaster County Historical Society (n.d.), *Asbury African Methodist Church*, Retrieved May 31, 2020, from http://sites.rootsweb.com/~paslchs/asburyamehis.html.

32. T. Hershberg (1974), Free Blacks in Antebellum Philadelphia, In E. Miller & E. Genovese, *Plantation, Town, and County: Essays on the Local History of American Slave Society* (Urbana: University of Illinois Press), pp. 415–40.

33. D. Porter (1995), *Early Negro Writing, 1760–1837* (Baltimore: Black Classic Press), p. 90.

34. Porter, *Early Negro Writing*, p. 295.

35. F. Lieber (1835), *The Stranger in America: Comprising Sketches of the Manners, Society, and National Peculiarities of the United States, in a Series of Letters to a Friend in Europe* (London: Richard Bentley, New Burlington Street), Retrieved July 13, 2020, from https://www.google.com/books/edition/The_Stranger_in_America/Q_ZBAQAA MAAJ?hl=en&gbpv=0.

36. D. Epstein (2003), *Sinful Tunes and Spirituals: Black Folk Music to the Civil War* (Urbana: University of Illinois Press), p. 223.

37. Turner, *Negro in Pennsylvania*, p. 127.

38. J. Horton & L. Horton (1997), *In Hope of Liberty; Culture, Community and Protest among Northern Free Blacks, 1700–1860* (New York: Oxford University Press), p. 96.

39. B. Arao (2016), *Roles of Black Women and Girls in Education: A Historical Reflection*, Retrieved May 31, 2020, from https://repository.usfca.edu/cgi/viewcontent .cgi?article=1012&context=listening_to_the_voices.

40. Porter, *Early Negro Writing*, p. 92.

41. Society of Friends (1849), *A Statistical Inquiry into the Condition of the People of Colour of the City and Districts of Philadelphia* (Philadelphia: Kite & Walton), Retrieved May 31, 2020, from https://www.google.com/books/edition/A_Statistical_Inquiry_Into_ the_Condition/B5YKJZxyTDsC?hl=en&gbpv=0.

42. F. Douglass (1853), *Letter to Harriet Beecher Stowe*, Retrieved August 9, 2020, from https://rbscp.lib.rochester.edu/4367.

43. C. Woodson (1919), *The Education of the Negro prior to 1861: A History of the Education of the Colored People of the United States from the Beginning of Slavery to the Civil War*, p. 310, Retrieved May 31, 2020, from https://www.google.com/books/edition/ The_Education_of_the_Negro_Prior_to_1861/U6sQAQAAMAAJ?hl=en&gbpv=0.

44. Lancaster County Historical Society (1849), *Lancaster Examiner and Herald, 1834–1854*, Retrieved May 31, 2020, from http://digitalcollections.powerlibrary.org/cdm/ compoundobject/collection/slchs-leh01/id/4421/rec/1.

45. National Assessment of Adult Literacy (n.d.), *120 Years of Literacy*, National Center for Education Statistics, Retrieved May 31, 2020, from https://nces.ed.gov/naal/ lit_history.asp.

46. A. Lloyd (2007), *Education, Literacy and the Reading Public*, Retrieved June 18, 2021, from https://www.gale.com/binaries/content/assets/gale-us-en/primary -sources/intl-gps/intl-gps-essays/full-ghn-contextual-essays/ghn_essay_bln_lloyd3_ website.pdf.

47. PA-Roots (n.d.), *25th Regiment, U.S. Colored Troops, Company A*, Retrieved May 31, 2020, from http://www.pa-roots.com/pacw/usct/25thusct/25thusctcoa.html.

48. W. Dobak (2011), *Freedom by the Sword: The U.S. Colored Troops, 1862–1867* (Washington, DC: Center of Military History, United States Army), pp. 62–64.

49. PA-Roots (n.d.), *3rd Regiment, U.S. Colored Troops, Company C*, Retrieved May 31, 2020, from http://www.pa-roots.com/pacw/usct/3rdusct/3rdusctcoc.html.

50. F. Douglass (1863), Why Should a Colored Man Enlist? *Douglass' Monthly*, Retrieved May 31, 2020, from University of Rochester, https://rbscp.lib.rochester .edu/4396.

51. W. Williams (2001), *Slavery and Freedom in Delaware 1639–1865* (Wilmington: SR Books), p. xvii.

52. Williams, *Slavery and Freedom in Delaware*, p. 189.

53. J. Futhey & G. Cope (1881), *History of Chester County, Pennsylvania, with Genealogical and Biographical Sketches* (Philadelphia: L. H. Everts), p. 266, https://

www.google.com/books/edition/History_of_Chester_County_Pennsylvania_w/
jcYxAQAAMAAJ?hl=en&gbpv=0.

54. E. Pinkowski (1962), *Chester County Place Names* (Philadelphia: Sunshine Press),
pp. 230–31.

55. Following a merger in 1866 with a Maryland offshoot of the African Methodist
Episcopal Church, the African Union Church is known today as the African Union
Methodist Protestant Church.

56. Williams, *Slavery and Freedom in Delaware*, p. 228.

57. Baldwin, *Invisible Strands in African Methodism*.

58. Baldwin, *Invisible Strands in African Methodism*.

59. R. Wright (1912), *The Negro in Pennsylvania: A Study in Economic History*
(Philadelphia: A.M.E. Book Concern Printers), p. 39, Retrieved June 21, 2021, from
https://hdl.handle.net/2027/yale.39002005397436.

60. Library of Congress (n.d.), *Colonization*, Retrieved July 13, 2020, from
https://www.loc.gov/exhibits/african/afam002.html#:~:text=The%20American%20
Colonization%20Society%20(ACS,the%20independent%20nation%20of%20Liberia.

61. Porter, *Early Negro Writing*, pp. 265–68.

62. D. Walker (1830), *Walker's Appeal, in Four Articles* (Boston: David Walker),
Retrieved July 1, 2021, from Documenting the American South, https://docsouth.unc
.edu/nc/walker/walker.html; emphasis original.

63. Wright, *Negro in Pennsylvania*, p. 39.

64. H. Bond (1976), *Education for Freedom: A History of Lincoln University, Pennsylvania* (Princeton: Princeton University Press), p. 151.

65. R. Butchart (2010), *Schooling the Freed People: Teaching, Learning, and the
Struggle for Black Freedom, 1861–1876* (Chapel Hill: University of North Carolina Press),
pp. 2, 19.

66. Butchart, *Schooling the Freed People*, p. 26.

67. I. Parker (1977), *The Rise and Decline of the Program of Education for Black Presbyterians of the United Presbyterian Church U.S.A., 1865–1970, Volume 5* (San Antonio:
Trinity University Press), p. 77.

68. W. Conser & R. Cain (2011), *Presbyterians in North Carolina: Race, Politics, and
Religious Identity in Historical Perspective* (Knoxville: University of Tennessee Press), p. 145.

69. P. Jones (1866), *Letter from Franklinton, North Carolina*, Retrieved August 6,
2020, from http://www.accessible.com/accessible.

70. General Book Steward's Correspondence (1866), *The Christian Recorder*, http://
www.accessible.com/accessible.

71. K. Zipf (1999), "The Whites Shall Rule the Land or Die": Gender, Race, and
Class in North Carolina Reconstruction Politics, *The Journal of Southern History*, 65(3),
pp. 499–534, https://doi.org/10.2307/2588132.

72. J. Crawford (1866), *North Carolina Correspondence. Franklinton, N.C.*, Retrieved
August 4, 2020, from https://accessible.com/accessible/emailedURL?AADoc=THECHRIS
TIANRECORDER.FR1866042109.73994.

73. North Carolina, Freedmen's Bureau (1866–1868), *North Carolina, Freedmen's
Bureau Assistant Commissioner Records, 1862–1870. Roll 11, Registered Letters Received,
Register 2, F-M, Nov 1866–Feb 1868*, Retrieved June 3, 2020, from http://www.ancestry
.com/interactive/61860/004567395_00021.

74. North Carolina (1870), *Public Laws of the State of North Carolina, Passed by
the General Assembly at Its Session 1869–70* (Raleigh: Jo. W. Holden, State Printer and

Binder), pp. xi, 422, 432, 445, 450, https://books.google.com/books?id=WJI4AAAAIAA
J&lpg=RA1-PA41&dq=public%20Laws%20of%20the%20State%20of%20North%20Caro
lina%2C%20Passed%20by%20the%20General%20Assembly%20at%20its%20Session%20
1869%E2%80%9370&pg=PP1#v=onepage&q=Crawford&f=false.

75. A. Trelease (1976), Republican Reconstruction in North Carolina: A Roll-Call
Analysis of the State House of Representatives, 1868–1870, *The Journal of Southern History 42*(3), p. 321, Retrieved August 30, 2020, from https://www.jstor.org/stable/2207155.

76. North Carolina Civil War Sesquicentennial (2020), *Reconstruction in North
Carolina*, Retrieved June 16, 2020, from http://www.nccivilwar150.com/history/recon
struction.htm.

77. J. Steele (2008), *A History of Second Presbyterian Church, Mocksville, NC*, North
Carolina Presbyterian Historical Society, Retrieved June 16, 2020, from http://www
.ncphsociety.org/newsletterWin08.html.

78. G. Muhammad (2012), The Literacy Development and Practices within African
American Literary Societies, *Black History Bulletin, 75*(1), pp. 6–13, Retrieved July 1,
2021, from http://www.jstor.org/stable/24759714.

79. E. McHenry (1995), *"Dreaded Eloquence": The Origins and Rise of African American Literary Societies and Libraries* (Cambridge: Harvard University Library), Retrieved
July 1, 2021, from http://nrs.harvard.edu/urn-3:HUL.InstRepos:42665394.

80. G. Patten (1912), The Seminole's Defiance, In J. Searson & G. Martin, *Studies in
Reading*, pp. 254–56, https://books.google.com/books?id=hdgAAAAAYAAJ&lpg
=PA254&ots=3_hs30grT5&dq=william%20g%20patte.

81. O. Edwards (2010), A Seminole Warrior Cloaked in Defiance. Retrieved July 13,
2020, from *Smithsonian Magazine*, https://www.smithsonianmag.com/history/a
-seminole-warrior-cloaked-in-defiance-60004300/.

82. Patten, Seminole's Defiance, pp. 254–56.

83. E. Wolf (1969), *Negro History 1553–1903* (Philadelphia: Library Company of Philadelphia), p. 57, Retrieved June 24, 2021, from https://www.google.com/books/edition/
Negro_History/f5wLch52LZ8C?hl=en&gbpv=0.

84. J. Winch (2000), *The Elite of Our People: Joseph Willson's Sketches of Black
Upper-Class Life in Antebellum Philadelphi*a (University Park: Pennsylvania State
University Press), p. 20.

85. US Census Bureau, *Social and Economic Status of the Black Population*, p. 61.

86. Du Bois, *Philadelphia Negro*, p. 145.

87. Winch, *Elite of Our People*, p. 101.

88. J. Horton (1993), *Free People of Color: Inside the African American Community*
(Washington, DC: Smithsonian Institution Press), p. 104.

89. S. Ruggles (1994), *The Origins of African-American Family Structure*, Retrieved
June 16, 2020, from http://users.hist.umn.edu/~ruggles/Articles/Af-Am-fam.pdf.

90. Lincoln University (1886/87), *Catalogue of Lincoln University, Chester County,
Pennsylvania, for the Academical Year, 1886–1887*, pp. 1–40, Retrieved June 16, 2020,
from https://archive.org/details/annualcatalogue8687linc.

91. Bond, *Education for Freedom*, p. 303.

92. Bond, *Education for Freedom*.

93. Winch, *Elite of Our People*, p. 101.

94. F. Douglass (1894), *Lessons of the Hour*, Retrieved June 16, 2020, from https://
archive.org/details/09359080.4757.emory.edu.

95. M. Terrell (1898), *The Progress of Colored Women* (Washington, DC: Smith Brothers), Retrieved June 16, 2020, from Gifts of Speech, http://gos.sbc.edu/t/terrell mary.html.

Epilogue

1. C. Schermerhorn (2019, June 19), Why the Racial Wealth Gap Persists, More than 150 Years after Emancipation, *The Washington Post*, https://www.washingtonpost.com/outlook/2019/06/19/why-racial-wealth-gap-persists-more-than-years-after-emancipation/.

2. F. Mitchell (2021), *New Data Show Stark Racial and Ethnic Differences in Young People's Healthy Development*, https://www.urban.org/urban-wire/new-data-show-stark-racial-and-ethnic-differences-young-peoples-healthy-development.

3. N. Bhutta, A. Chang, L. Dettling, J. Hsu, & J. Hewitt (2020), *Disparities in Wealth by Race and Ethnicity in the 2019 Survey of Consumer Finances.* Board of Governors of the Federal Reserve System, https://www.federalreserve.gov/econres/notes/feds-notes/disparities-in-wealth-by-race-and-ethnicity-in-the-2019-survey-of-consumer-finances-20200928.htm.

4. W. Collins & M. Wanamaker (2021), *African American Intergenerational Economic Mobility since 1880*, p. 4, Retrieved July 1, 2021, from http://www.nber.org/papers/w23395.

5. E. Badger, C. Miller, A. Pearce, & K. Quealy (2018), Extensive Data Shows Punishing Reach of Racism for Black Boys, *New York Times*, https://www.nytimes.com/interactive/2018/03/19/upshot/race-class-white-and-black-men.html.

6. Committee on the Negro "Call" for a National Conference (1909), *NAACP: A Century in the Fight for Freedom: Founding and Early Years*, Retrieved from Library of Congress, http://www.loc.gov/exhibits/naacp/founding-and-early-years.html.

7. Du Bois, *Souls of Black Folk*, p. 4.

Bibliography

Abbott, L., & Seroff, D. (2002). *Out of Sight: The Rise of African American Popular Music, 1889–1895*. Jackson: University Press of Mississippi.

Abbott, L., & Seroff, D. (2012 reprint). *Ragged but Right: Black Traveling Shows, "Coon Songs," and the Dark Pathway to Blues and Jazz*. Jackson: University Press of Mississippi.

Advertisement. (1909, February 14). *The Daily Ardmoreite*. Retrieved May 26, 2020, from Library of Congress, Chronicling America, https://chroniclingamerica.loc.gov/lccn/sn85042303/1909-02-14/ed-1/seq-7/.

Africa! The Colored Population of Philadelphia. (1867, March 30). *The Evening Telegraph* (Philadelphia). Retrieved July 13, 2020, from Library of Congress, Chronicling America: https://chroniclingamerica.loc.gov/lccn/sn83025925/1867-03-30/ed-1/seq-1/.

African Methodist Episcopal Church. (n.d.). *Our History*. Retrieved June 18, 2021, from https://www.ame-church.com/our-church/our-history/.

Anderson, A. (2000). *Snake Oil, Hustlers and Hambones: The American Medicine Show*. Jefferson, NC: McFarland. https://www.google.com/books/edition/Snake_Oil_Hustlers_and_Hambones/FRSBCgAAQBAJ?hl=en&gbpv=1&dq=Ann+Anderson+Snake+Oil,+Hustlers+and+Hambones&printsec=frontcover.

Apel, D. (2007). Lynching Photographs and Public Shaming. In D. Apel, & S. M. Smith, *Lynching Photographs* (pp. 42–78). Berkeley: University of California Press.

Arao, B. (2016). *Roles of Black Women and Girls in Education: A Historical Reflection*. Retrieved May 31, 2020, from https://repository.usfca.edu/cgi/viewcontent.cgi?article=1012&context=listening_to_the_voices.

Ater, R. (2011). *Remaking Race and History: The Sculpture of Meta Warrick Fuller*. Berkeley: University of California Press.

The Atlanta Massacre. (1906, September 29). *The Indianapolis Freeman*, p. 4. Retrieved April 18, 2020, from http://news.google.com/newspapers?nid=FIkAGs9z2eEC&dat=19060929&printsec=frontpage&hl=en.

The Atlantic City Experience. (2020). *The Atlantic City Experience*, http://www.atlanticcityexperience.org/index.php?option=com_content&view=article&id=10:northside-atlantic-city- black-community&catid=7&Itemid=11.

Attitude of White Press. (1908, April 4). *The Indianapolis Freeman*, p. 6. Retrieved June 18, 2021, from https://news.google.com/newspapers?nid=FIkAGs9z2eEC&dat=19080404&printsec=frontpage&hl=en.

Badger, E., Miller, C. C., Pearce, A., & Quealy, K. (2018, March 19). Extensive Data Shows Punishing Reach of Racism for Black Boys. *New York Times*. https://www.nytimes.com/interactive/2018/03/19/upshot/race-class-white-and-black-men.html.

Baldwin, J. (1963). *The Fire Next Time*. New York: Dial Press.

Baldwin, L. V. (1983). *"Invisible" Strands in African Methodism: A History of the African Union Methodist Protestant and Union American Methodist Episcopal Churches,*

1805–1980. Metuchen, NJ: American Theological Library Association, and London: Scarecrow Press.

The Bancroft Library. (2006). *The 1906 San Francisco Earthquake and Fire*. Retrieved May 26, 2020, from https://bancroft.berkeley.edu/collections/earthquakeandfire/exhibit/room03.html.

Barnes, R. L. (2016). *Darkology: The Hidden History of Amateur Blackface Minstrelsy and the Making of Modern America, 1860–1970*. Retrieved May 18, 2021, from Harvard Library, Office for Scholarly Communication: https://dash.harvard.edu/handle/1/33493592.

Bassett, F. (n.d.). *Wish You Were Here! The Story of the Golden Age of Picture Postcards in the United States*. New York State Library, Manuscripts and Special Collections. Retrieved April 18, 2020, from http://www.nysl.nysed.gov/msscfa/qc16510ess.htm.

Bergman, P. M. (1969). *The Chronological History of the Negro in America*. New York: Harper & Row.

Berkeley School of Information. (n.d.). *About South Hall*. Retrieved April 14, 2018, from https://www.ischool.berkeley.edu/about/southhall.

Bhutta, N., Chang, A. C., Dettling, L. J., Hsu, J. W., & Hewitt, J. (2020, September 28). *Disparities in Wealth by Race and Ethnicity in the 2019 Survey of Consumer Finances*. Retrieved from Board of Governors of the Federal Reserve System, https://www.federalreserve.gov/econres/notes/feds-notes/disparities-in-wealth-by-race-and-ethnicity-in-the-2019-survey-of-consumer-finances-20200928.htm.

The Bluefield Evening Leader. Advertisement. (1910, January 22). Retrieved May 15, 2020, from Library of Congress, Chronicling America: https://chroniclingamerica.loc.gov/lccn/sn86092066/1910-01-22/ed-1/seq-7/.

Bodnar, J. E. (1997). "The Impact of the "New Immigration" on the Black Worker: Steelton, Pennsylvania, 1880–1920." In J. Trotter, & E. Smith (Eds.), *African Americans in Pennsylvania: Shifting Historical Perspectives* (pp. 257–71). Harrisburg: The Pennsylvania Historical and Museum Commission and University Park: The Pennsylvania State University Press.

Bolster, W. J. (1997). *Black Jacks: African American Seamen in the Age of Sail*. Cambridge: Harvard University Press.

Bond, H. M. (1976). *Education for Freedom: A History of Lincoln University, Pennsylvania*. Princeton: Princeton University Press.

[Booker T. Washington]. (n.d.). [Photograph]. Library of Congress. *Prints & Photographs Online Catalogue*. Retrieved April 20, 2020, from https://memory.loc.gov/pnp/cph/3a40000/3a49000/3a49600/3a49671r.jpg.

Boston University. (2015, October 8). *William Keylor in City Journal: Wilson's Racism*. Retrieved April 21, 2020, from https://www.bu.edu/pardeeschool/2015/10/08/william-keylor-in-city-journalwilsons-racism/.

Bouton, T. (n.d.) *Slave, Free Black, and White Population, 1780–1830*. Department of History, University of Mayland Baltimore County. Retrieved May 31, 2020, from https://userpages.umbc.edu/~bouton/History407/SlaveStats.htm.

Boyd's Chester County, Pennsylvania Directory. (1896–97). Philadelphia: C. E. Howe. https://www.ancestry.com/search/collections/10689/.

Brooks, D. E., & Hébert, L. P. (2006). Gender, Race, and Media Representation. In B. J. Dow, & J. T. Wood, *The SAGE Handbook of Gender and Communication* (pp. 297–318). Thousand Oaks, CA: SAGE. Retrieved May 28, 2021, from https://us.corwin.com/sites/default/files/upm-binaries/11715_Chapter16.pdf.

Bruce, D. D. (1989). *Black American Writing from the Nadir: The Evolution of a Literary Tradition, 1877–1915*. Baton Rouge: Louisiana State University Press.

Butchart, R. E. (2010). *Schooling the Freed People: Teaching, Learning, and the Struggle for Black Freedom, 1861–1876*. Chapel Hill: University of North Carolina Press.

Christmas Frolics at the White House from the Time of Washington to the Present Day. (1913, December 21). *The Evening Star* (Washington, DC). Retrieved April 21, 2020, from Chronicling America: Historic American Newspapers, https://chroniclin gamerica.loc.gov/lccn/sn83045462/1913-12-21/ed-1/seq-55/.

City of San Bernardino California. (n.d.). *About San Bernardino*. Retrieved May 26, 2020, from http://www.sbcity.org/about/default.asp.

City of Tumwater, Washington. (2020, July 13). *About Tumwater: History*. Retrieved July 13, 2020, from https://www.ci.tumwater.wa.us/about-tumwater/history#:~:tex t=When%20the%20City%20was%20founded,other%20points%20on%20Puget%20 Sound.

Clark, K. R. (2008, November 9). *Shasta Springs—Forgotten Resort*. Retrieved July 13, 2020, from http://shastasprings.com/Resort/.

Clark-Lewis, E. (1994). *Living In, Living Out: African American Domestics in Washington, D.C., 1910–1940*. Washington, DC: Smithsonian Institution Press.

The Coconino Sun. Untitled article. (1906, February 10). Retrieved August 10, 2020, from Library of Congress, Chronicling America, https://chroniclingamerica.loc.gov/lccn/ sn87062055/1906-02-10/ed-1/seq-3/.

Cohan, G. M. *The Man in the Moon Is a Coon*. New York: Howley, Haviland. Retrieved from Southern Illinois University Library, https://doi.org/10.5479/sil.982148.mq168 7926.

Collins, W. J., & Wanamaker, M. H. (2021, April). African American Intergenerational Economic Mobility since 1880. *NBER Working Paper Series*. Retrieved July 1, 2021, from http://www.nber.org/papers/w23395.

Colorado Encyclopedia. (n.d.). *Tabor Grand Opera House*. Retrieved May 12, 2020, from https://coloradoencyclopedia.org/article/tabor-grand-opera-house.

The Colored American Magazine. (1900, May). Editorial and Publisher's Announcements, p. 61. Retrieved August 10, 2020, from https://babel.hathitrust.org/cgi/pt?id=uc1.b379 3660&view=2up&seq=72&q1=the%20south%20is%20attempting.

Committee on the Negro "Call" for a National Conference. (1909). *NAACP: A Century in the Fight for Freedom: Founding and Early Years*. Retrieved from Library of Congress, http://www.loc.gov/exhibits/naacp/founding-and-early-years.html.

Comstock House. (2013). *On Tuesday the Monster Came to Town*. Retrieved May 26, 2020, from http://comstockhousehistory.blogspot.com/2013/02/on-tuesday-mon ster-came-to-town.html.

Conser, W. H., & Cain, R. J. (2011). *Presbyterians in North Carolina: Race, Politics, and Religious Identity in Historical Perspective*. Knoxville: University of Tennessee Press.

The Coon Caricature. (n.d.). Jim Crow Museum of Racist Memorabilia. Ferris State University. Retrieved July 2, 2021, from https://www.ferris.edu/jimcrow/coon/.

Crawford, J. H. (1866, April 7). North Carolina Correspondence. Franklinton, N.C. *The Christian Recorder*. Retrieved August 4, 2020, from Accessible Archives, https:// accessible.com/accessible/emailedURL?AADoc=THECHRISTIANRECORDER .FR1866042109.73994.

Crouthamel, J. L. (1960, July). The Springfield Race Riot of 1908. *Journal of Negro History* 45(3), 65–81. Retrieved April 18, 2020, from http://www.jstor.org/stable/2716259.

Davis, J. A. (2014). Variety Shows, Minstrelsy, and Social Aesthetics during the Virginia Encampment of 1863–64. *The Virginia Magazine of History and Biography, 122*(2), 128–55. Retrieved May 28, 2021, from http://www.jstor.org/stable/24393923.

Densmore, C. (n.d.). *Quakers and the Underground Railroad: Myths and Realities.* Retrieved April 20, 2020, from http://web.tricolib.brynmawr.edu/speccoll/quaker sandslavery/commentary/organizations/underground_railroad.php.

Deserts Heir to Riches on Her Way to the Altar. (1907, November 7). *The News-Democrat* (Providence, RI). Retrieved from http://news.google.com/newspapers?id=TCB bAAAAIBAJ&sjid=0E4NAAAAIBAJ&pg=1076,4223046&dq=wilson-howe&hl=en.

DeVan, Kathryn. (2008). *Our Most Famous Border: The Mason-Dixon Line.* Retrieved July 13, 2020, from Pennsylvania Center for the Book, https://www.pabook.libraries .psu.edu/literary-cultural-heritage-map-pa/feature-articles/our-most-famous -border-mason-dixon-line.

Dickens, C. (1913). *American Notes for General Circulation.* London: Chapman & Hall. Retrieved April 29, 2020, from Project Gutenberg, https://www.gutenberg.org/ files/675/675-h/675-h.htm.

Digital Public Library of America. (1922). *A Draft Eulogy Written by W.E.B. Du Bois about Bert Williams.* Retrieved May 22, 2021, from https://dp.la/primary-source -sets/blackface-minstrelsy-in-modern-america/sources/1436.

Dobak, W. A. (2011). *Freedom by the Sword: The U.S. Colored Troops, 1862–1867.* Washington, DC: Center of Military History, United States Army.

Douglass, F. (1848). *Address at the Celebration of West India Emancipation, Rochester, N.Y.* Retrieved May 29, 2020, from Library of Congress, https://www.loc.gov/resource/ mfd.21023/?sp=4&st=single.

Douglass, F. (1894). *Lessons of the Hour.* Retrieved June 16, 2020, from https://archive .org/details/09359080.4757.emory.edu.

Douglass, F. (1853, March 8). Letter to Harriet Beecher Stowe. Retrieved August 9, 2020, from Frederick Douglass Project, University of Rochester, https://rbscp.lib.rochester .edu/4367.

Douglass, F. (1863, April). Why Should a Colored Man Enlist? *Douglass' Monthly.* Retrieved May 31, 2020, from Frederick Douglass Project, University of Rochester, https://rbscp.lib.rochester.edu/4396.

Du Bois, W. E. B. (1900, June 29). *The American Negro at Paris.* Retrieved June 27, 2021, from http://www.webdubois.org/dbANParis.html.

Du Bois, W. E. B. (1900). *The College-Bred Negro: Report of a Social Study Made under the Direction of Atlanta University.* Retrieved July 18, 2020, from https://www.goo gle.com/books/edition/The_College_bred_Negro/qm42AAAAMAAJ?hl=en &gbpv=0.

Du Bois, W. E. B. (1911, January). Editorial. Colored Men Lynched without Trial, *The Crisis 1*(3), p. 26, retrieved from Modernist Journals Project, https://modjourn.org/ issue/bdr507847/.

Du Bois, W. E. B. (1911, June). Editorial. *The Crisis, 2*(2), 63. Retrieved June 28, 2021, from Modernist Journals Project, modjourn.org/issue/bdr522172/.

Du Bois, W. E. B. (1934, March 13). *A Negro Nation within a Nation.* Retrieved April 18, 2020, from https://www.blackpast.org/african-american-history/1934-w-e-b-du -bois-negro-nation-within-nation/.

Du Bois, W. E. B. (1913). *Open Letter to Woodrow Wilson.* Retrieved April 21, 2020, from https://teachingamericanhistory.org/library/document/open-letter-to-woodrow-wilson/.

Du Bois, W. E. B. (1899). *The Philadelphia Negro: A Social Study*. New York: Schocken Books. Reprint ed. 1994.

Du Bois, W. E. B. (1903). *The Souls of Black Folk*. New York: Dover. Retrieved April 18, 2020, from https://www.gutenberg.org/files/408/408-h/408-h.htm.

Du Bois, W. E. B. (1898). *Some Efforts of American Negroes for Their Own Social Betterment. Report of an Investigation under the Direction of Atlanta University; Together with the Proceedings of the Third Conference for the Study of the Negro Problems, Held at Atlanta University*. Retrieved April 18, 2020, from Documenting the American South, University of North Carolina, https://docsouth.unc.edu/church/duboisau/dubois.html.

Du Bois, W. E. B., & Dill, A. G. (1914). *Morals and Manners among Negro Americans*. Atlanta: Atlanta University Publications.

Dunbar, P. L. (1895). *We Wear the Mask*. Retrieved May 22, 2021, from poetryfoundation.org/poems/44203/we-wear-the-mask.

Eaton, I. (1899). Special Report on Negro Domestic Service in the Seventh Ward, Philadelphia. In W. E. B. Du Bois, *The Philadelphia Negro: A Social Study*. New York: Schocken.

Edwards, G., & Cobb, W. (1901). *I'll Be with You When the Roses Bloom Again*. Retrieved July 20, 2020, from SecondHandSongs, https://secondhandsongs.com/work/130096/all.

Edwards, O. (2010, October). A Seminole Warrior Cloaked in Defiance. Retrieved July 13, 2020, from *Smithsonian Magazine*, https://www.smithsonianmag.com/history/a-seminole-warrior-cloaked-in-defiance-60004300/.

Ellis, F., & Evans, S. (1883). *History of Lancaster County, Pennsylvania: With Biographical Sketches of Many of Its Pioneers and Prominent Men*. Philadelphia: Everts & Peck. https://www.google.com/books/edition/History_of_Lancaster_County_Pennsylvania/yX7IhoEQUaQC?hl=en&gbpv=0.

Ellis, N. (2020, February 25). Descendants. *The Washington Post*. https://www.washingtonpost.com/nation/2020/02/25/lost-lineage-quest-identify-black-americans-roots/?arc404=true.

Ellison, R. (2011). *The Collected Essays of Ralph Ellison*. New York: Modern Library. https://www.google.com/books/edition/The_Collected_Essays_of_Ralph_Ellison/GT3oSgZKvQoC?hl=en&gbpv=1&dq=the+collected+essays+of+ralph+ellison&printsec=frontcover.

Emery, L. F. (1988). *Black Dance from 1619 to Today, Second Edition*. Trenton, NJ: Princeton Book Company.

Epstein, D. J. (2003). *Sinful Tunes and Spirituals: Black Folk Music to the Civil War*. Urbana: University of Illinois Press.

Facing History and Ourselves. (n.d.). *The Reconstruction Acts of 1867*. Retrieved April 18, 2020, from https://www.facinghistory.org/reconstruction-era/reconstruction-acts-1867.

Fiorellini, N. (2020, August 3). Statue of White Woman Holding Hatchet and Scalps Sparks Backlash in New England. *The Guardian*. https://www.theguardian.com/us-news/2020/aug/03/hannah-duston-statue-new-hampshire-native-americans.

Foner, E. (2020, February 26). *Reconstruction*. Retrieved April 18, 2020, from https://www.britannica.com/event/Reconstruction-United-States-history.

Fort Worth Telegram. (1907, May 2). *The Waxahachie Daily Light*, Waxahachie, Texas, p. 2. Retrieved June 17, 2021, from Library of Congress, Chronicling America: https://chroniclingamerica.loc.gov/lccn/sn86090369/1907-05-02/ed-1/seq-2/.

Foster, F. S. (2008). *Love and Marriage in Early African America*. Boston: Northeastern University Press.

Foster, S. (1848). *Old Uncle Ned*. Retrieved May 12, 2020, from Song of America, https://songofamerica.net/song/old-uncle-ned/.

The Friends Meeting. (1915). *Two Hundredth Anniversary of the Establishment of The Friends Meeting at New Garden, Chester County*. Retrieved April 12, 2021, from Pennsylvania: https://www.ancestry.com/search/collections/10661/.

Futhey, J. S., & Cope, G. (1881). *History of Chester County, Pennsylvania, with Genealogical and Biographical Sketches*. Philadelphia: L. H. Everts. https://www.google.com/books/edition/History_of_Chester_County_Pennsylvania_w/jcYxAQAAMAAJ?hl=en&gbpv=0.

Gannett, H. (1895). *Occupations of the Negroes*. Baltimore: The Trustees. Retrieved June 11, 2021, from https://hdl.handle.net/2027/nnc2.ark:/13960/t6qz65x3h?urlappend=%3Bseq=8.

General Book Steward's Correspondence. (1866, March 31). *The Christian Recorder*. Retrieved from Accessible Archives, http://www.accessible.com/accessible.

George Mason University. (n.d.). *Booker T. Washington Delivers the 1895 Atlanta Compromise Speech*. Retrieved April 18, 2020, from History Matters, http://historymatters.gmu.edu/d/39/.

The Georgia Minstrels. (1906, September 27). *Daily Capital Journal*. Retrieved May 22, 2020, from Library of Congress, Chronicling America, https://chroniclingamerica.loc.gov/lccn/sn99063957/1906-09-27/ed-1/seq-6/.

Gibson, R. A. (n.d.). *Booker T. Washington and W. E. B. Du Bois: The Problem of Negro Leadership*. Retrieved April 18, 2020, from https://teachersinstitute.yale.edu/curriculum/units/1978/2/78.02.02.x.html.

The Great Ferdon Co. No. 2. (1908, September 19). *The Indianapolis Freeman*, p. 5. Retrieved July 21, 2020, from https://news.google.com/newspapers?nid=FIkAGs9z2eEC&dat=19080919&printsec=frontpage&hl=en.

Ham, D. N. (1993). *The African-American Mosaic: A Library of Congress Resource Guide for the Study of Black History and Culture*. Washington, DC: Library of Congress.

Harley, S. (1978). Northern Black Female Workers: Jacksonian Era. In S. Harley, & R. Terborg-Penn (Eds.), *The Afro-American Woman* (pp. 5–16). Port Washington, NY: Kennikat Press.

Harper, D. (2003). *Race Relations in Pennsylvania*. Retrieved May 31, 2020, from Slavery in the North. http://slavenorth.com/pennrace.htm.

Harper, D. (2003). *Slavery in Pennsylvania*. Retrieved May 31, 2020, from Slavery in the North. http://slavenorth.com/pennsylvania.htm.

Harris, M. L. (1899, June 29). *Negro Womanhood*. Retrieved April 18, 2020, from Public Opinion. https://www.google.com/books/edition/Public_Opinion/SIY-AQAAMAAJ?hl=en&gbpv=1&dq=Negro+womanhood.+Mrs.+L.+H.+Harris.&pg=PA812&printsec=frontcover.

Hassan, A. (2018, February 24). A Postcard View of African-American Life. *The New York Times*. https://www.nytimes.com/2018/02/24/us/a-postcard-view-of-african-american-life.html.

Hatanaka, R. (2019, June 18). *Streetcars before Buses: British Columbia Electric Railway*. Retrieved May 26, 2020, from University of British Columbia, Digitization Centre, https://digitize.library.ubc.ca/digitizers-blog/streetcars-before-buses-british-columbia-electric-railway/.

Hearn, M. (2013, July 18). *Saucy Postcards: The Bamforth Collection*. London: Little, Brown Book Group Limited. https://www.google.com/books/edition/Saucy_Postcards_The_Bamforth_Collection/bq2aDwAAQBAJ?hl=en&gbpv=0.

Hershberg, T. (1974). Free Blacks in Antebellum Philadelphia. In E. Miller, & E. D. Genovese (Eds.), *Plantation, Town, and County: Essays on the Local History of American Slave Society* (pp. 415–40). Urbana: University of Illinois Press.

Hewitt, W. L. (1991) Wicked Traffic in Girls: Prostitution and Reform in Sioux City, 1885–1910. *The Annals of Iowa 51*(2), pp. 123–48. doi: https://doi.org/10.17077/0003-4827.9577.

Historic Kennett Square. (n.d.). *Kennett Square Walking Tour*. Retrieved February 15, 2020, from https://historickennettsquare.com/about/history/walking-tour/.

The Historical Marker Database. (2019, October 25). *The John A. Wilson Building*. Retrieved July 13, 2020, from Historical Marker Database, https://www.hmdb.org/m.asp?m=65712.

The History of Esko and Thomson Township. (2016, July 22). Retrieved May 22, 2020, from http://www.eskohistory.com/gallery/image/762211/3383851.

History of Minstrelsy. (n.d.). *Ragtime and the "Coon Song."* Retrieved May 12, 2020, from http://exhibits.lib.usf.edu/exhibits/show/minstrelsy/jimcrow-to-jolson/ragtime-and-the-coon-song.

History.com. (2021, January 25). *NAACP*. Retrieved May 18, 2021, from https://www.history.com/topics/civil-rights-movement/naacp.

Hobbs, F., & Stoops, N. (2002). *Demographic Trends in the 20th Century*. Washington, DC: US Census Bureau.

Hopkins, L. (2000, July 6). *Among These Hills: African Americans in Lancaster County's Southern End*. Presentation to the Southern Lancaster County Historical Society.

Horton, J. O. (1993). *Free People of Color: Inside the African American Community*. Washington, DC: Smithsonian Institution Press.

Horton, J. O., & Horton, L. E. (1997). *In Hope of Liberty; Culture, Community and Protest among Northern Free Blacks, 1700–1860*. New York: Oxford University Press.

Hudson, L. M. (2008). Entertaining Citizenship: Masculinity and Minstrelsy in Post-Emancipation San Francisco. *The Journal of African American History*, *93*(2), 174–97. http://www.jstor.org/stable/25609967.

Hurley, M. (1997). *The Average Yearly Salaries of All Industries Excluding Farm Labor*. Retrieved April 20, 2020, from Bryant University, https://web.bryant.edu/~ehu/h364proj/sprg_97/hurley/salary.html.

The Idaho Springs Sifting-News. (1906, September 1). Retrieved July 14, 2020, from Library of Congress, Chronicling America, https://chroniclingamerica.loc.gov/lccn/sn90051006/1906-09-01/ed-1/seq-4/.

Illinois Health News. (1912). *Illinois Health News; Volume 8*. https://www.google.com/books/edition/Illinois_Health_News/4wIgAQAAMAAJ?hl=en&gbpv=0.

I's A-Waiting for You, Josie. (n.d.). Retrieved May 22, 2020, from https://monologues.co.uk/musichall/Songs-I/Is-Awaiting-For-You-Josie.htm.

Isaacs, E. J. (1947). *The Negro in the American Theatre*. New York: Theatre Arts.

Janken, K. R. (2001). Introduction. In W. White, *Rope and Faggot; A Biography of Judge Lynch* (pp. vii–xxv). Notre Dame: University of Notre Dame Press.

Jaspin, E. (2018, September 26). Leave or Die: America's Hidden History of Racial Expulsions. *Austin-American Statesman*. https://www.statesman.com/news/20161014/leave-or-die-americas-hidden-history-of-racial-expulsions.

Jim Crow: A Comic Song Sung by Mr. Rice at the Chestnut St. Theatre. (1832). Philadelphia: J. Edgar. Edison Collection of American Sheet Music. https://hdl.handle.net/2027/mdp.39015096384907?urlappend=%3Bseq=2%3Bownerid=114188231-1.

Jim Crow Museum of Racist Memorabilia. (n.d.). Ferris State University. Retrieved May 12, 2020, from https://ferris.edu/jimcrow/.

Johns Hopkins University. (n.d.). *The Thompson Street Cadets. The Latest, The Greatest, Sure Hit, The Best Coon March Song Published.* Retrieved August 10, 2020, from https://images.app.goo.gl/RhVRomB6cTkXKabc7

Johnson, N. (2010). *The Northside: African Americans and the Creation of Atlantic City.* Medford: Plexus.

Jones, J. A. (1999). *Remarks on Racial and Cultural Conflict in Chester County for the Discussion of the 1845 Edition of the Narrative of the Life of Frederick Douglass, an American Slave.* Retrieved May 31, 2020, from https://digitalcommons.wcupa.edu/cgi/viewcontent.cgi?article=1053&context=hist_wchest.

Jones, P. J. (1866, May 5). Letter from Franklinton, North Carolina. *The Christian Recorder.* Retrieved August 6, 2020, from Accessible Archives, http://www.accessible.com/accessible.

J. T. McCaddon Arrested: American Whose Circus Failed Accused of Fraudulent Bankruptcy. (1905, October 1). *The New York Times*, p. 2. https://timesmachine.nytimes.com/timesmachine/1905/10/01/101331270.html?pageNumber=2.

Juravich, T., Hartford, W. F., & Green, J. R. (1996). *Commonwealth of Toil: Chapters in the History of Massachusetts Workers and Their Unions.* Amherst: University of Massachusetts Press.

Kornacki, J. (2015). General Strike of 1910. In *The Encyclopedia of Greater Philadelphia*, https://philadelphiaencyclopedia.org/archive/general-strike-of-1910/.

Lafrance, A. (2016, October 26). "The Weird Familiarity of 100-Year-Old Feminism Memes." *The Atlantic.* Retrieved February 17, 2020, from https://www.theatlantic.com/technology/archive/2016/10/pepe-the-anti-suffrage-frog/505406/.

Lancaster County Historical Society. (1849, March 28). *Lancaster Examiner and Herald, 1834–1854.* Retrieved May 31, 2020, from Lancaster History.org, http://digitalcollections.powerlibrary.org/cdm/compoundobject/collection/slchs-leh01/id/4421/rec/1.

Lee, A. W. (2007). Introduction. In D. Apel, & S. M. Smith, *Lynching Photographs* (pp. 1–9). Berkeley: University of California Press.

Leetaru, K. (2011). *Mechanical Engineering Shop Laboratory/Wood Shop and Foundry Laboratory.* Retrieved May 26, 2020, from UIHistories Project: A History of the University of Illinois, http://uihistories.library.illinois.edu/cgi-bin/cview?SITEID=1&ID=280.

Leon, C. B. (2016). *The Life of American Workers in 1915.* Retrieved January 30, 2020, from US Bureau of Labor Statistics, https://www.bls.gov/opub/mlr/2016/article/the-life-of-american-workers-in-1915.htm.

Lerner, G. (1974, April). Early Community Work of Black Club Women. *The Journal of Negro History, 59*(2), 158–67. Retrieved July 25, 2020, from https://www.jstor.org/stable/2717327.

Levine, L. W. (1977). *Black Culture and Black Consciousness.* New York: Oxford University Press.

Lewis, Cary B. (1908, December 26). Race Progress! Louisville and Her Host of Thriving Afro-American Citizens. *The Indianapolis Freeman*, p. 2. Retrieved July 2, 2021, from https://news.google.com/newspapers?nid=FIkAGs9z2eEC&dat=19081226&printsec=frontpage&hl=en.

Lewis, R. M. (2007). *From Traveling Show to Vaudeville: Theatrical Spectacle in America, 1830–1910*. Baltimore: Johns Hopkins University Press. https://www.google.com/books/edition/From_Traveling_Show_to_Vaudeville/ijl-W-QoacMC?hl=en&gbpv=1&dq=From%20Traveling%20Show%20to%20Vaudeville%3A%20Theatrical%20Spectacle%20in%20America%2C%201830-1910&pg=PA1&printsec=frontcover&bsq=From%20Traveling%20Show%.

Lewis, W. D. (2003). *A Brief History of African American Marching Bands*. Retrieved May 12, 2020, from Folkstreams, http://www.folkstreams.net/film-context.php?id=249.

Library of Congress. (n.d.). *African American Timeline: 1850 to 1925*. Retrieved April 18, 2020, from Library of Congress, https://www.loc.gov/collections/african-american-perspectives-rare-books/articles-and-essays/timeline-of-african-american-history/1901-to-1925/.

Library of Congress. (n.d.). *Colonization*. Retrieved July 13, 2020, from Library of Congress, The African-American Mosaic, https://www.loc.gov/exhibits/african/afam002.html#:~:text=The%20American%20Colonization%20Society%20(ACS,the%20independent%20nation%20of%20Liberia.

Library of Congress. (n.d.). *Rise of Industrial America, 1876–1900*. Retrieved April 18, 2020, from http://www.loc.gov/teachers/classroommaterials/presentationsandactivities/presentations/timeline/riseind/.

Lieber, F. (1835). *The Stranger in America: Comprising Sketches of the Manners, Society, and National Peculiarities of the United States, in a Series of Letters to a Friend in Europe*. London: Richard Bentley, New Burlington Street. Retrieved July 13, 2020, from https://www.google.com/books/edition/The_Stranger_in_America/Q_ZBAQAAMAAJ?hl=en&gbpv=0.

Lincoln University. (1886/87). *Catalogue of Lincoln University, Chester County, Pennsylvania, for the Academical Year, 1886–1887*. Retrieved June 16, 2020, from https://archive.org/details/annualcatalogue8687linc.

Lincoln University. (1918). *Lincoln University College and Theological Seminary: Biographical Catalogue 1918*. Lancaster: The New Era Printing Company. Retrieved April 25, 2020, from http://www.lincoln.edu/library/specialcollections/alumnimagazine/1918.pdf.

Lincoln University. (1909). *Lincoln University Herald*. Lincoln University, Pennsylvania. Retrieved April 25, 2020, from Lincoln University, https://www.lincoln.edu/sites/default/files/library/specialcollections/herald/1909.pdf.

Lititz Public Library. (n.d.). *Historical African American Churches in Lancaster County*. Retrieved May 31, 2020, from https://lititzlibrary.org/historical-african-american-churches-in-lancaster-county/.

Little, B. (2019, April 12). *How the Galveston Hurricane of 1900 Became the Deadliest U.S. Natural Disaster*. Retrieved May 26, 2020, from History.com, https://www.history.com/news/how-the-galveston-hurricane-of-1900-became-the-deadliest-u-s-natural-disaster.

Litwack, L. F. (1998). *Trouble in Mind: Black Southerners in the Age of Jim Crow*. New York: Alfred E. Knopf.

Lloyd, A. J. (2007). *Education, Literacy and the Reading Public*. Gale Primary Sources. Retrieved June 18, 2021, from https://www.gale.com/binaries/content/assets/gale-us-en/primary-sources/intl-gps/intl-gps-essays/full-ghn-contextual-essays/ghn_essay_bln_lloyd3_website.pdf.

Logan, R. W. (1954). *The Negro in American Life and Thought: The Nadir, 1877–1901*. New York: Dial Press.

Malloy, M. (1990). *African Americans in the Maritime Trades: A Guide to Resources in New England.* Sharon, MA: Kendall Whaling Museum. Retrieved July 12, 2021, from Kendall Whaling Museum Monograph Series (No. 6), https://www.whalingmuseum .org/sites/default/files/pdf/KWM%20Monograph%20Series%20No%206_African%20 Americans.pdf.

Maloney, T. N. (2002, January 14). *African Americans in the Twentieth Century.* Economic History Association. Retrieved April 18, 2020, from https://eh.net/ encyclopedia/african-americans-in-the-twentieth-century/.

McGill, R. (1965, November). *The Atlantic Online: W. E. B. DuBois.* https://www.theat lantic.com/past/docs/unbound/flashbks/black/mcgillbh.htm.

McHenry, E. (1995). *"Dreaded Eloquence": The Origins and Rise of African American Literary Societies and Libraries.* Cambridge: Harvard University Library. Retrieved July 1, 2021, http://nrs.harvard.edu/urn-3:HUL.InstRepos:42665394.

Meier, A. (1963). *Negro Thought in America, 1880–1915: Racial Ideologies in the Age of Booker T. Washington.* Ann Arbor: University of Michigan Press.

Merritt, C. (2008). *Something So Horrible: The Springfield Race Riot of 1908.* Retrieved April 18, 2020, from https://www.illinois.gov/alplm/museum/Education/Docu ments/Race_Riot_Catalog_2008.pdf.

Mitchell, F. (2021, February 22). *New Data Show Stark Racial and Ethnic Differences in Young People's Healthy Development.* Retrieved from Urban Wire, https://www .urban.org/urban-wire/new-data-show-stark-racial-and-ethnic-differences-young -peoples-healthy-development.

MonopolyCity.com. (2008). *Early Hotels—From Atlantic City's Nostalgic Past.* https:// www.monopolycity.com/ac_earlyhotels.html.

Montgomery, L. M. (1908). *Anne of Green Gables.* Retrieved April 25, 2020, from https://www.gutenberg.org/files/45/45-h/45-h.htm.

Morton, P. (1991). *Disfigured Images: The Historical Assault on Afro-American Women.* New York: Praeger.

Muhammad, G. E. (2012, Winter/Spring). The Literacy Development and Practices within African American Literary Societies. *Black History Bulletin, 75*(1), 6–13. Retrieved July 1, 2021, from http://www.jstor.org/stable/24759714.

NAACP. (2008, August 12). *NAACP Leaders Mark 100th Anniversary of Springfield Race Riot.* https://www.naacp.org/latest/naacp-leaders-mark-100th-anniversary-of -springfield-race-riot/.

Nash, G. B. (1991). *Freedom by Degrees: Emancipation in Pennsylvania and Its After- math.* New York: Oxford University Press USA.

National Assessment of Adult Literacy. (n.d.). *120 Years of Literacy.* National Center for Education Statistics. Retrieved May 31, 2020, from https://nces.ed.gov/naal/lit_his tory.asp.

NationMaster. (n.d.). *Economy > GDP per Capita in 1900: Countries Compared.* Retrieved April 18, 2020, from https://www.nationmaster.com/country-info/stats/ Economy/GDP-per-capita-in-1900.

Negro Slays Officer: Citizens Meet and Order Many Blacks to Leave Town. (1907, April 27). *Bryan Morning Eagle.* Retrieved June 17, 2021, from Library of Congress, Chron- icling America: https://chroniclingamerica.loc.gov/lccn/sn86088652/1907-04-27/ ed-1/seq-2.

Negroes Were Mobbed. (1909, November 2). *Palestine, Texas, Daily Herald.* (1909, November 2). Retrieved May 15, 2020, from Library of Congress, Chronicling Amer- ica, https://chroniclingamerica.loc.gov/lccn/sn86090383/1909-11-02/ed-1/seq-1/.

New Bedford Whaling Museum. (2018, February 20). *African-Americans in New Bedford*. Retrieved May 31, 2020, from https://www.whalingmuseum.org/learn/research-topics/cultural-communities#African-Americans%20in%20NB.

North Carolina. (1870). *Public Laws of the State of North Carolina, Passed by the General Assembly at Its Session 1869–70*. Raleigh: Jo. W. Holden, State Printer and Binder. https://books.google.com/books?id=WJI4AAAAIAAJ&lpg=RA1-PA41&dq=public%20Laws%20of%20the%20State%20of%20North%20Carolina%2C%20Passed%20by%20the%20General%20Assembly%20at%20its%20Session%201869%E2%80%9370&pg=PP1#v=onepage&q=Crawford&f=false.

North Carolina Civil War Sesquicentennial. (2020). *Reconstruction in North Carolina*. Retrieved June 16, 2020, from http://www.nccivilwar150.com/history/reconstruction.htm.

North Carolina, Freedmen's Bureau. (1866–1868). *North Carolina, Freedmen's Bureau Assistant Commissioner Records, 1862–1870. Roll 11, Registered Letters Received, Register 2, F-M, Nov 1866–Feb 1868*. Retrieved June 3, 2020, from Ancestry.com, http://www.ancestry.com/interactive/61860/004567395_00021.

Not Pity but Respect. (1906, May). *Alexander's Magazine*, pp. 18–19, https://hdl.handle.net/2027/inu.30000117863757?urlappend=%3Bseq=27.

Notable Kentucky African Americans. (2018, August 27). *African American Schools in Christian County, Kentucky*. Retrieved May 26, 2020, from http://nkaa.uky.edu/nkaa/items/show/2649.

Notes from Al. E. Holman's Band and Serenaders, Now Touring Europe with the J. T. McCaddon's Company. (1905, May 6). *The Indianapolis Freeman*, p. 5. Retrieved May 15, 2020, from https://news.google.com/newspapers?nid=FIkAGs9z2eEC&dat=19050506&printsec=frontpage&hl=en.

Office for Civil Rights, US Dept. of Education. (1991, March). *Historically Black Colleges and Universities and Higher Education Desegregation*. Retrieved April 18, 2020, from https://www2.ed.gov/about/offices/list/ocr/docs/hq9511.html.

Old Comedian Dead (1915, July 1), *Artesia Pecos Valley News*, https://newspaperarchive.com/other-articles-clipping-jul-01-1915-229432/.

Osborne, L. B. (2003). Introduction. In T. L. Congress, *A Small Nation of People: W. E. B. Du Bois & African American Portraits of Progress* (pp. 13–20). New York: Amistad.

Otfinoski, S. (2003). *African Americans in the Visual Arts*. New York: Facts on File, Inc. Retrieved July 2, 2021, from https://www.google.com/books/edition/African_Americans_in_the_Visual_Arts/BcWHdpRoDkUC?hl=en&gbpv=1&bsq=battey.

Padgett, K. (n.d.). *Blackface! Minstrel Show Female Impersonators*. Retrieved May 28, 2021, from https://black-face.com/minstrel-female-impersonators.htm.

Palmer, T. S. (1897). *The Jack Rabbits of the United States*. Washington, DC: Government Printing Office. https://books.google.com/books?id=t9ArAAAAYAAJ&ppis=_e&printsec=frontcover&source=gbs_ge_summary_r&cad=0#v=onepage&q&f=false.

Parker, I. M. (1977). *The Rise and Decline of the Program of Education for Black Presbyterians of the United Presbyterian Church U.S.A., 1865–1970, Volume 5*. San Antonio: Trinity University Press.

PA-Roots. (n.d.). *3rd Regiment, U.S. Colored Troops, Company C*. Retrieved May 31, 2020, from http://www.pa-roots.com/pacw/usct/3rdusct/3rdusctcoc.html.

PA-Roots. (n.d.). *25th Regiment, U.S. Colored Troops, Company A*. Retrieved May 31, 2020, from http://www.pa-roots.com/pacw/usct/25thusct/25thusctcoa.html.

Patten, G. (1912). The Seminole's Defiance. In J. Searson, & G. Martin, *Studies in Reading* (pp. 254–56). Chicago: University Publishing Company. Retrieved from https://books .google.com/books?id=hdgAAAAAYAAJ&lpg=PA254&ots=3_hs30grT5&dq=william %20g%20patte.

PBS. (n.d.). *The African Americans: Many Rivers to Cross*. Retrieved April 20, 2020, from Racist Images and Messages in Jim Crow Era. https://www.pbs.org/video/ african-americans-many-rivers-cross-racist-images-and-messages-jim-crow-era/.

Pennsylvania Historical & Museum Commission. (2015, August 26). *Historic Agricultural Resources of Pennsylvania c 1700–1960*. Retrieved April 25, 2020, from Pennsylvania Agricultural History Project. http://www.phmc.state.pa.us/portal/ communities/agriculture/history/index.html.

Pennsylvania Society for Promoting the Abolition of Slavery. (1838). *The Present State and Condition of the Free People of Color, of the City of Philadelphia*. Retrieved May 29, 2020, from https://archive.org/details/presentstatecondoopenn.

Philadelphia Area Archives Research Portal. (n.d.). *Conard-Pyle Company Records*. Retrieved July 13, 2020, from http://dla.library.upenn.edu/dla/pacscl/ead.html?id =PACSCL_UDel_UDelMSS634.

Philadelphia Zoo Gatehouses. (n.d.). Retrieved April 8, 2018, from https://philly.curbed .com/maps/best-frank-furness-projects-philadelphia/philadelphia-zoo-gatehouses.

Pickaninny Mine, Come Hide Away. (1899). Retrieved January 11, 2022, from Library of Congress, Performing Arts Databases, http://memory.loc.gov/diglib/ihas/loc.award .rpbaasm.0855/default.html.

Pinkowski, E. (1962). *Chester County Place Names*. Philadelphia: Sunshine Press.

Porter, D. (1995). *Early Negro Writing, 1760–1837*. Baltimore: Black Classic Press.

Princeton University. (n.d.). *McCaddon Collection of the Barnum and Bailey Circus 1871–1907*. Retrieved May 15, 2020, from Princeton University Library Manuscripts Division, http://arks.princeton.edu/ark:/88435/02870v897.

Race Feeling Grows Intense. (1906, April 17). *Augusta Chronicle* (Augusta, Georgia). Retrieved August 10, 2020, from https://augustachronicle.newsbank.com/search ?text=race%20feeling%20grows%20intense&content_added=&date_from=&date_ to=&pub%5B0%5D=1252FEAF2D2D3A44.

Richards & Pringle's Minstrels: Holland & Filkings, Mgrs. (1909, July 31). *Indianapolis Freeman*, p. 5. Retrieved July 21, 2020, from https://news.google.com/ newspapers?nid=FIkAGs9z2eEC&dat=19090731&printsec=frontpage&hl=en.

Riis, T. L. (1989). *Just Before Jazz: Black Musical Theater in New York, 1890–1915*. Washington, DC: Smithsonian Institution.

Route (Richards & Pringle's Minstrels). (1910, April 2). *The Indianapolis Freeman*, p. 5. Retrieved June 11, 2021, from https://news.google.com/newspapers?nid=FIkAG s9z2eEC&dat=19100402&printsec=frontpage&hl=en.

Ruggles, S. (1994, February). *The Origins of African-American Family Structure*. Retrieved June 16, 2020, from http://users.hist.umn.edu/~ruggles/Articles/Af -Am-fam.pdf.

Russell, S. (1909, August 7). Opening of the Georgia Minstrels. *The Indianapolis Freeman*, p. 6. Retrieved May 26, 2020, from https://news.google.com/ newspapers?nid=FIkAGs9z2eEC&dat=19090807&printsec=frontpage&hl=en.

Russo, M. H. (2005). *Hinsonville, a Community at the Crossroads: The Story of a Nineteenth-Century African-American Village*. Selinsgrove, PA: Susquehanna University Press.

Ryan, D. B. (1982). *Picture Postcards in the United States, 1893–1918*. New York: Potter.

Sampson, H. T. (1988). *The Ghost Walks: A Chronological History of Blacks in Show Business, 1865–1910.* London: Scarecrow Press.

Santa Monica History Museum. (2020). *Santa Monica History.* Retrieved July 13, 2020, from https://santamonicahistory.org/santa-monica-history/.

Schermerhorn, C. (2019, June 19). Why the Racial Wealth Gap Persists, More than 150 Years after Emancipation. *The Washington Post.* https://www.washingtonpost.com/outlook/2019/06/19/why-racial-wealth-gap-persists-more-than-years-after-emancipation/.

Semuels, A. (2016, July 22). The Racist History of Portland, the Whitest City in America. *The Atlantic.* https://www.theatlantic.com/business/archive/2016/07/racist-history-portland/492035/.

Shane, C. (2011, April 15). Why the Dearth of Statues Honoring Women in Statuary Hall and Elsewhere? *The Washington Post.* https://www.washingtonpost.com/lifestyle/style/why-the-dearth-of-statues-honoring-women-in-statuary-hall-and-elsewhere/2011/04/11/AFx8lgjD_story.html.

Simpson, M. (2004, March). Archiving Hate: Lynching Postcards at the Limit of Social Circulation. *ESC: English Studies in Canada 30*(1), 17–38. Retrieved July 2, 2021, from Johns Hopkins University, https://muse.jhu.edu/article/689499/pdf.

Smith, E. L. (1998). The End of Black Voting Rights in Pennsylvania: African Americans and the Pennsylvania Constitutional Convention of 1837–1838. *Pennsylvania History 65*(3), 279–99. Retrieved May 31, 2020, from https://www.jstor.org/stable/27774118.

Smith, J. E. (2008). *FDR.* New York: Random House.

Society of Friends. (1849). *A Statistical Inquiry into the Condition of the People of Colour of the City and Districts of Philadelphia.* Philadelphia: Kite & Walton. Retrieved May 31, 2020, from https://www.google.com/books/edition/A_Statistical_Inquiry_Into_the_Condition/B5YKJZxyTDsC?hl=en&gbpv=0.

Soderlund, J. R. (1983, January). Black Women in Colonial Pennsylvania. *The Pennsylvania Magazine of History and Biography 107*(1), 49–68. Retrieved July 12, 2021, from https://www.jstor.org/stable/20091739.

Sorin, G. (2020). *Driving While Black: African American Travel and the Road to Civil Rights.* New York: Liveright.

South Carolina. (1907, April 27). *New York Dramatic Mirror,* p. 8.

Southern Lancaster County Historical Society. (n.d.). *Asbury African Methodist Church.* Retrieved May 31, 2020, from http://sites.rootsweb.com/~paslchs/asburyamehis.html.

Southern, E. (1996). The Georgia Minstrels: The Early Years. In A. J. Bean, *Inside the Minstrel Mask: Readings in 19th-Century Blackface Minstrelsy* (pp. 163–75). Hanover, NH: Wesleyan University Press.

Southern, E. (1997). *The Music of Black Americans, Third Edition.* New York: W. W. Norton.

St. Cloud State University. (n.d.). *History and Traditions.* Retrieved May 26, 2020, from https://www.stcloudstate.edu/studenthandbook/history-traditions.aspx.

Steele, J. L. (2008). *A History of Second Presbyterian Church, Mocksville, NC.* Retrieved June 16, 2020, from the North Carolina Presbyterian Historical Society, http://www.ncphsociety.org/newsletterWin08.html.

Strain, E. (2003). *Public Places, Private Journeys: Ethnography, Entertainment, and the Tourist Gaze.* New Brunswick, NJ: Rutgers University Press.

Sturcke, J. (2009, February 5). Golliwog Began as Beloved Children's Character. *The Guardian,* https://www.theguardian.com/world/2009/feb/05/golliwog-history-florence-kate-upton.

Taylor, R. J., Chatters, L. M., Woodward, A. T., & Brown, E. (2013). *Racial and Ethnic Differences in Extended Family, Friendship, Fictive Kin and Congregational Informal Support Networks*. Retrieved April 21, 2020, from US National Library of Medicine, https://www.ncbi.nlm.nih.gov/pmc/articles/PMC4116141/.

Terrell, M. C. (1898, February 18). *The Progress of Colored Women*. Washington, DC: Smith Brothers. Retrieved June 16, 2020, from Gifts of Speech, http://gos.sbc.edu/t/terrellmary.html.

Toll, R. C. (1974). *Blacking Up: The Minstrel Show in 19th-Century America*. London: Oxford University Press.

Trelease, A. W. (1976, August). *Republican Reconstruction in North Carolina: A Roll-Call Analysis of the State House of Representatives, 1868–1870. The Journal of Southern History 42*(3), 319–44. Retrieved August 30, 2020, from https://www.jstor.org/stable/2207155.

Tuck DB Postcards. (n.d.). *History of Raphael Tuck & Sons LTD*. Retrieved July 13, 2020, from https://tuckdbpostcards.org/history.

Turner, E. R. (1969). *The Negro in Pennsylvania: Slavery—Servitude—Freedom, 1639–1861*. New York: Negro Universities Press.

Tyson, R. (n.d.). *Our First Friends, the Quakers*. Retrieved April 20, 2020, from Pennsylvania Heritage, http://www.phmc.state.pa.us/portal/communities/pa-heritage/our-first-friends-early-quakers.html.

Tzeng, T. (2011, January 1). Eastern Promises: The Role of Eastern Capital in the Development of Los Angeles, 1900–1920. *California History 88*(2), 32–61, https://doi.org/10.2307/23052268.

University of Saskatchewan. (n.d.). *Ambisextrous: Gender Impersonators of Music Hall and Vaudeville*. Retrieved May 28, 2021, from http://digital.scaa.sk.ca/gallery/genderimpersonators/.

US Census Bureau. (1980). *The Social and Economic Status of the Black Population in the United States: An Historical View, 1790–1978*. Special Studies, P-Series. Report No. 23–80. Washington, DC: US Census Bureau, Current Population Reports.

Walker, D. (1830). *Walker's Appeal, in Four Articles*. Boston: David Walker. Retrieved July 1, 2021, from Documenting the American South, https://docsouth.unc.edu/nc/walker/walker.html.

Wang, A.B., & Sonmez, F. (2022, March 29). Biden Signs Bill Making Lynching a Federal Hate Crime. *The Washington Post*. https://www.washingtonpost.com/politics/2022/03/29/biden-signs-bill-lynching-hate-crime/.

Ward, N. (2016). *A Brief History of the Pantomime – And Why It's About So Much More than "Blokes in Dresses."* Retrieved February 26, 2022, from https://theconversation.com/a-brief-history-of-the-pantomime-and-why-its-about-so-much-more-than-blokes-in-dresses-69683.

Washington, B. T. (1896, September). The Awakening of the Negro. *The Atlantic*. Retrieved September 20, 2020, from https://www.theatlantic.com/magazine/archive/1896/09/the-awakening-of-the-negro/305449/.

Washington, B. T. (1908). Wants Justice for Negro: Booker T. Washington Makes Another Plea. (1908, August 29). *The Indianapolis Freeman*, p. 1. Retrieved April 18, 2020, from https://news.google.com/newspapers?nid=FIkAGs9z2eEC&dat=19080829&printsec=frontpage&hl=en.

Watt, P. D. (2017). *Cheap Print and Popular Song in the Nineteenth Century*. Cambridge: Cambridge University Press. Retrieved May 22, 2020, from https://books.google.com/books?id=V3U3DgAAQBAJ&dq=song+i%27se+a+waiting+for+you+josie&source=gbs_navlinks_s.

W. E. B. (William Edward Burghardt) Du Bois, 1868–1963. (n.d.). [Photograph]. Library of Congress. Prints & Photographs Online Catalogue. Retrieved April 20, 2020, from W. E. B. (William Edward Burghardt) Du Bois, 1868–1963: http://loc.gov/pictures/resource/cph.3a53178/.

Wendell, S. (1990, Autumn). Oppression and Victimization; Choice and Responsibility. *Hypatia* 5(3), 15–46. Retrieved July 10, 2021, from https://www.jstor.org/stable/3809974.

Wichita Falls, Texas. (n.d.). *A Very Short History of Wichita Falls.* Retrieved May 26, 2020, from https://tx-wichitafalls3.civicplus.com/DocumentCenter/View/19746/Very-Short-History-of-WF?bidId=.

Wife of Woodrow Wilson's Nephew Found Dead. (April 12, 1928.) *Border Cities Star* (Windsor, Ontario), p. 1. Retrieved April 21, 2020, https://news.google.com/newspapers?id=ScFEAAAAIBAJ&sjid=OroMAAAAIBAJ&pg=1693,3626684&dq=virgini.

Williams, W. H. (2001). *Slavery and Freedom in Delaware 1639–1865.* Wilmington: SR Books.

Willis, D. (2003). The Sociologist's Eye: W. E. B. Du Bois and the Paris Exposition. In T. L. Congress, *A Small Nation of People: W. E. B. Du Bois & African American Portraits of Progress* (pp. 51–78). New York: Amistad.

Winch, J. (2000). *The Elite of Our People: Joseph Willson's Sketches of Black Upper-Class Life in Antebellum Philadelphia.* University Park: Pennsylvania State University Press.

Wolf, E. I. (1969). *Negro History 1553–1903.* Philadelphia: Library Company of Philadelphia. Retrieved June 24, 2021, from https://www.google.com/books/edition/Negro_History/f5wLch52LZ8C?hl=en&gbpv=0.

Woodson, C. G. (1919). *The Education of the Negro prior to 1861: A History of the Education of the Colored People of the United States from the Beginning of Slavery to the Civil War.* Retrieved May 31, 2020, from https://www.google.com/books/edition/The_Education_of_the_Negro_Prior_to_1861/U6sQAQAAMAAJ?hl=en&gbpv=0.

Work, M. N. (1913). *Fifty Years of Negro Progress* 6(10). Washington, DC: Associated Publishers, Inc. Retrieved June 11, 2021, from https://hdl.handle.net/2027/emu.10002331968?urlappend=%3Bseq=7.

Wormser, R. (n.d.). *The Rise and Fall of Jim Crow.* Retrieved February 10, 2022, from https://www.thirteen.org/wnet/jimcrow/index.html.

Wright, R. R. (1912). *The Negro in Pennsylvania: A Study in Economic History.* Philadelphia: A.M.E. Book Concern Printers. Retrieved June 21, 2021, from https://hdl.handle.net/2027/yale.39002005397436.

Wright Realtors. (n.d.). *Stockton Midtown Houses.* Retrieved April 21, 2020, from https://www.wrightrealtors.com/stockton/houses-midtown.htm.

Vintage Golliway soft toy. Karen Arnold, CC0, via Wikimedia Commons: https://commons.wikimedia.org/wiki/File:Vintage-golliway-soft-toy.jpg.

Yeomans, C. (2018, January 27). Piece of History Lost after Jones Bridge Collapses into Chattahoochee River. *Gwinnett Daily Post.* https://www.gwinnettdailypost.com/local/piece-of-history-lost-after-jones-bridge-collapses-into-chattahoochee/article_1354b1b8-24c8-59fe-8bed-f3712d88b091.html.

Zipf, K. L. (1999, August). "The Whites Shall Rule the Land or Die": Gender, Race, and Class in North Carolina Reconstruction Politics. *The Journal of Southern History* 65(3), pp. 499–534. https://www.jstor.org/stable/2588132?origin=crossref.

Index

About the Author

Photo by Archie J. Brown

Faith Mitchell has a PhD in medical anthropology from the University of California, Berkeley, and in a career of several decades has bridged research, philanthropy, and social and health policy. She is currently an Institute Fellow at the Urban Institute in Washington, DC.

In addition to writing and editing numerous policy-related publications, Faith is the author of *Hoodoo Medicine*; *Gullah Herbal Remedies*, a groundbreaking study of African American folk medicine, and *The Book of Secrets, Part 1*, a supernatural novel. She is active on numerous professional boards and committees related to her interests in improving health policy and advancing racial justice. She and her husband, Archie, live in Northern Virginia.

ma why
write to me.
our photo.
wishes.
ma.
Sister.
ford.
d. co.
Cal.

19[?] [?]
'08
CAL.

1706 FRANKLIN [?]
POSTAGE
ONE CENT

Miss Emma V. Crawford.

Malvern,
To John T. Haines,
Chester Co.,
Pennsylvania.

203798. [?]